James Levi

Rising Above Your Hurt to Greatness

The Story of Jephthah:
Son of a Prostitute, A Mighty Warrior

James Levi, Ph.D.

Cover design: Lifexcel Leadership

Published by: Lifexcel Leadership

P.O Box 953 Huntsville, Texas 77342

For Worldwide Distribution, Printed in the U.S.A.

1 2 3 4 5 6 /18 17 16 15

All rights reserved.

For more information please contact: Lifexcel Leadership at lifexcelleadershipseries@gmail.com

ISBN- 978-1-7344551-7-5

DEDICATION

This book is dedicated to those going through homelessness of their souls due to deep wounds and hurts. Yet they know deep in their hearts that God has called them to be warriors fighting those battles for greatness.

James Levi

CONTENTS

ACKNOWLEDGMENTS

Once again, I am grateful for a fantastic team of professionals who helped me put this book together. Foremost is my publisher at Lifexcel Publishing. I also appreciate the designing and marketing teams for their hard work.

In this book, I gather stories that I've heard from my friends and people whom I have met around the world. I value their roles and encouragement. Thanks to all who have touched my life with their own. My desire in writing this book is to help you see what God is doing in, around and through you, so we can become blessings to bring glory to God.

I am grateful to my wife Annie and our children Saakshi and Namrata, who are my source of daily inspiration.

James Levi

Judges 11

Jephthah the Gileadite was a mighty warrior. His father was Gilead; his mother was a prostitute.2 Gilead's wife also bore him sons, and when they were grown up, they drove Jephthah away. "You are not going to get any inheritance in our family," they said, "because you are the son of another woman." 3 So Jephthah fled from his brothers and settled in the land of Tob, where a gang of scoundrels gathered around him and followed him. 4 Sometime later, when the Ammonites were fighting against Israel, 5 the elders of Gilead went to get Jephthah from the land of Tob. 6 "Come," they said, "be our commander, so we can fight the Ammonites." 7 Jephthah said to them, "Didn't you hate me and drive me from my father's house? Why do you come to me now, when you're in trouble?" 8 The elders of Gilead said to him, "Nevertheless, we are turning to you now; come with us to fight the Ammonites, and you will be head over all of us who live in Gilead." 9 Jephthah answered, "Suppose you take me back to fight the Ammonites and the Lord gives them to me—will I really be your head?" 10 The elders of Gilead replied, "The Lord is our witness; we will certainly do as you say." 11 So Jephthah went with the elders of Gilead, and the people made him head and commander over them. And he repeated all his words before the Lord in Mizpah. Then Jephthah sent messengers to the Ammonite king with the question: "What do you have against me that you have attacked my country?" 13 The king of the Ammonites answered Jephthah's messengers, "When Israel came up out of Egypt, they took away my land from the Arnon to the Jabbok, all the way to the Jordan. Now give it back peaceably." 14 Jephthah sent back messengers to the Ammonite king, 15 saying: "This is what Jephthah says: Israel did not take the land of Moab or the land of the Ammonites. 16 But when they came up out of Egypt, Israel went through the wilderness to the Red Sea and on to Kadesh. 17 Then Israel sent messengers to the king of Edom, saying, 'Give us permission to go through your country,' but the king of Edom would not listen. They sent also to the king of Moab, and he refused. So, Israel stayed at Kadesh. 18 "Next, they traveled through the wilderness, skirted the lands of Edom and Moab, passed along the eastern side of the country of Moab, and camped on the other side of the Arnon. They did not enter the territory of Moab, for the Arnon was its border. 19 "Then Israel sent messengers to Sihon king of the Amorites, who ruled in Heshbon, and said to him, 'Let us pass through your country to our own place.' 20 Sihon, however, did not trust Israel[b] to pass through his territory. He mustered all his troops and encamped at Jahaz and fought with Israel. 21 "Then the Lord, the God of Israel, gave Sihon and his whole army into Israel's hands, and they defeated them. Israel took over all the land of the Amorites who lived in that country, 22 capturing all of it from the Arnon to the Jabbok and from the desert to the Jordan. 23 "Now since the Lord, the God of Israel, has driven the Amorites out before his people Israel, what right have you to take it over? 24 Will you not take what your god Chemosh gives you? Likewise, whatever the Lord our God has given us, we will possess. 25 Are you any better than Balak son of Zippor, king of Moab? Did he ever quarrel with Israel or fight with them? 26 For three hundred years Israel occupied Heshbon, Aroer, the surrounding settlements and all the towns along the Arnon. Why didn't you retake them during that time? 27 I have not wronged you, but you are doing me wrong by waging war against me. Let the Lord, the Judge, decide the dispute this day between the Israelites and the Ammonites." 28 The king of Ammon, however, paid no attention to the message Jephthah sent him.29 Then the Spirit of the Lord came on Jephthah. He crossed Gilead and Manasseh, passed through Mizpah of Gilead, and from there he advanced against the Ammonites. 30 And Jephthah made a vow to the Lord: "If you give the Ammonites into my hands, 31 whatever comes out of the door of my house to meet me when I return in triumph from the Ammonites will be the Lord's, and I will sacrifice it as a burnt offering." 32 Then Jephthah went over to fight the Ammonites, and the Lord gave them into his hands. 33 He devastated twenty towns from Aroer to the vicinity of Minnith, as far as Abel Keramim. Thus, Israel subdued Ammon. 34 When Jephthah returned to his home in Mizpah, who should come out to meet him but his daughter, dancing to the sound of timbrels! She was an only child. Except for her he had neither son nor daughter.35 When he saw her, he tore his clothes and cried, "Oh no, my daughter! You have brought me down and I am devastated. I have made a vow to the Lord that I cannot break." 36 "My father," she replied, "you have given your word to the Lord. Do to me just as you promised, now that the Lord has avenged you of your enemies, the

Ammonites. 37 But grant me this one request," she said. "Give me two months to roam the hills and weep with my friends, because I will never marry." 38 "You may go," he said. And he let her go for two months. She and her friends went into the hills and wept because she would never marry. 39 After the two months, she returned to her father, and he did to her as he had vowed. And she was a virgin. From this comes the Israelite tradition 40 that each year the young women of Israel go out for four days to commemorate the daughter of Jephthah the Gileadite.

Introduction

Who are you?

What is going on within your soul?

Are you chasing your past?

How do you escape the mess that you were born into?

Living in the present cannot be easy when you are burdened with your past. Depending on the circumstances, it could become more challenging to carry on as time passes. Not everyone is born with a stigma or social bias or within a system that inherently works against them, but still, we all carry the pains, hurts, and sins of our past.

Sometimes we do not know how to unburden

ourselves of it. So, we stay stuck in a cycle of shame, abuse, or self-harm. And after a while, that unhealthy cycle becomes so normal that we can't imagine a life outside of it.

If you are a child of abuse or neglect, you did not create or willingly participate in some of the things that defined your developing years—yet the consequences of other people's actions are still a part of your everyday life. It may seem as though you didn't sin, yet you have become a sinner. You may feel like you have to carry the burden of your *"father's sin"* to your grave. You cannot just shake it off and move on with your life because it is way more than you can fix on your own, and maybe the truth is that you, like Jephthah, exist because of your *father's sin*. Now you are tied to all that is happening around you or even to you because of someone else's actions that may have occurred before your birth.

How can one untangle that?

How deep is the wound that you cannot hide from, run from, or live with?

What do you do at such a time in your life? Is there a

way out from this homelessness of one's soul?

The ancient text offers comfort to the weary; the Scripture here offers a grand promise to those who have lost their way. It guides us to move beyond the circumstances surrounding us and help us to grasp hold of our true identity and achieve the greatness that each of us is created for. This is the story of connecting to our holy significance and true purpose, which allows us that opportunity to disconnect ourselves from every mistake that has tried to hold us hostage, bring us down, or cage us in an attempt to prevent us from moving forward to experience the life that is genuinely rich and abundant, as God has promised to us.

I invite you onto a journey through the life of a man named Jephthah, who rose above one of the most challenging circumstances life can throw at anyone and thus lived a life greater than him, bringing deliverance to his community and people at large. He reached that place in history to achieve the immensity and might only God could render.

This may seem impossible to many, yet it came true for an ordinary man—one who had been driven away from his own home and wandered around as a homeless man because he didn't belong among his brothers. In his story, we see the reason that propelled him to rise above the challenges and face those stormy, life-threatening situations to become a leader: a man of influence. All this he achieved even when there were the obstacles of weakness, flaws, and the same human fear that any normal human being would have. But still, he made it.

So, you can make it too!

I encourage you to walk with me as we watch this mighty warrior—the son of a prostitute—in his rejection, in his pain, in his confusion, in his struggles, in his insecurities, in his fear, and in his faith in a God who is passionately pursuing each of us so that we might know and find ourselves in Him. There we find our purpose, our life, and greatness.

1

Son of a Prostitute

Jephthah the Gileadite was a mighty warrior. His father was Gilead; his mother was a prostitute. Gilead's wife also bore him sons, and when they were grown up, they drove Jephthah away. "You are not going to get any inheritance in our family," they said, "because you are the son of another woman."—Judges 11:1–2

She was one of the kindest humans ever to walk the halls of Jones Middle School. Most teachers praised how she exemplified kindness and humility in the real world. Martha Robinson was her name, and she lived up to every expectation, day after day, without ever failing or fumbling. It all seemed to come naturally to her as she moved through the day with apparent ease, composure, and peace. There was never a day she didn't reach out to help someone in the school who was going through a difficult time. They say she had an instinct for knowing who was hurting or who was in pain by just being around people. Then she would sit with that person, listening and offering the kindest words of encouragement, often while holding their hands. On rare occasions, she would be seen wiping their tears as she held her fellow students to her shoulders.

Though everyone admired her ability, no one knew her. Though she was there for many, none were there to understand why an eleven-year-old would behave in such an out-of-the-ordinary and mature way. It was, and still is, an implausible way for someone of her age to be carrying others' burdens and messes on her tiny and tender shoulders.

Then one day, everything changed. Her unknown past was revealed, and the goodwill others held for her evaporated like a vapor on a hot day.

Unknown to the school, Martha came from a troubled home. She kept the details of her life secret out of fear and a desire to protect her family. But then, in a rare moment of her overwhelmed soul crying out for the same compassion she lavished on others, she confessed and told everything about her and her life to one of her best friends.

What others had lived in ignorance of for years, this best friend of hers made known in just a moment. As this news spread from student to student and then to the teachers, everyone discovered who Martha Robinson was behind her mask of kindness. It also gave everyone the opportunity and freedom to ridicule and spit on the now-soiled reputation of an 11-year-old girl.

Her crime was being the daughter of an alcoholic and single father who frequented the county jail more often than one goes to the grocery store. She had two younger siblings, twins less than three years old. Her mother had died giving birth to the twins, depriving the children of the primary breadwinner of the family and the one who brought some stability at home.

Martha's father was rarely home as he was battling his long-term addiction to alcohol. Though he'd fought his way to sobriety for a time, the death of his wife sent him back to the bottle with abandon. In addition to neglect, her father physically abused them when the drink overtook his senses.

The children were often left on their own; thus, all responsibility fell on the shoulders of Martha. At that young age, when others went to games and movies or were with their friends, she cooked, cleaned, and often consoled her younger siblings when they had to go to bed without food. There were times when the authorities tried to intervene and take the children away. Still, Martha had been sincerely praying and telling the lies her father told her to tell the authorities so that her family would be kept together.

Until her secret was revealed, no one looking at Martha, how she handled life, and how she would take others' problems upon herself would have ever suspected the hell she was living in at home.

After Martha's friend shared her story, the one place she felt safe in the world became yet another place of abuse. Children who had formerly been friends began avoiding her because their parents did want the evil influence of a child from such a troubled home to rub off on them. She became the object of ridicule among the rest of the students. And those she'd formerly comforted abandoned her in her grief.

The situation worsened when the school principal informed the officials to move in to take the children away from their father, which ultimately separated Martha and her twin siblings. The long-term effects of this exposure affected her health and emotional condition for years. She would complain about severe abdominal pain and sickness, often miss classes, and could be found resting at the nurse's station. This small haven also relieved her from bullying and gossiping that followed her everywhere she went.

The nurse, a kind older woman, loved her unconditionally and encouraged her to look up above her situation to see the beauty in her. She also reminded Martha that the brokenness of her life, which everyone expected to be her destruction, could become a catalyst that would allow her to go further in life than her classmates living in comfort and casting stones at her (for the crime of being the daughter of a man controlled by his own demons).

It didn't make much sense to her then, but Martha, who has now become a well-known author and speaker, credits her small interactions with that nurse with being the reason she came out of the trauma in her life to experience true greatness.

How often do we live the pain and shame caused by the sin and judgment of others? How often do we judge people because of their *father's sin*, even though they bear no personal blame?

Living the *father's sin: His father was Gilead... —Judges 11:1*

The story of Jephthah began when his father slept with a prostitute that bore him a son. His *father's sin* was that he wanted more than what he had. He had a wife at home. Yet he went out to someone to get something he thought he needed or deserved. That affair also gifted him with a son. The time with the prostitute may have been pleasurable, exotic, and comforting for a moment, but what happened through that relationship was neither noble nor exciting. His act brought shame to him and his family. It led to division among his sons. And it resulted in a child his family would outright reject for the sin of being born of another woman.

Many of us carry some form of such heaviness that we are unaware of. For some of us, it may not be the result of our *father's sin*, but something society deems unsavory that may have been passed on through another familial connection. Those labels and wounds become part of us, seemingly a curse that cannot be broken or overcome. It can be challenging to move forward in boldness or confidence when our identities are formed and framed by the actions of others.

Though it may feel like there is no clear way to work around the misguided opinions of others (or to move beyond the actions that have been committed against you or that have come to define you), though you are innocent of the sin, we are promised that our God is faithful. He will walk us through those dark valleys into a place where we can eat and rest in peace, even while we are surrounded by enemies who speak lies about us or seek to harm us.

The father's Sin: It is something you have no part in, but you live with the shame of it all your life, or that follows you, shapes, and often cripples you. It doesn't have to involve your father (like in the case of Jephthah) or your parents or even your family, but it could be hurt that you received because of someone else's mistake or crime. The *father's sin* can be a stain that never leaves you, and you can never clean yourself thoroughly off it, often taking its echoing consequences to the grave.

Your *father's sin* may have shaped your early life but remember this: You are not responsible for his failings before or after you were born. Yes, the consequences of his actions may have colored your view of yourself and played a part in your decisions. Still, those wounds and acts have also played a crucial role in developing the character you need to become someone who rises above the expectations and condemnation of others. Often, it would be almost impossible to separate your past from yourself because that separation would erase your existence. Without those experiences, you would not be you.

So, what do you do? What is the best option for those

living out the consequences of someone else's wrong choices?

I recently met with a bank manager who confessed to his years of struggle with a similar issue. Upon closely probing his family situation, I discovered that he grew up in a decent home where his parents were engaging and affirming. Both were good people who loved their children and provided them with a good education that helped the son get an excellent job at a bank. The trouble was that he joined the bank during an enormous scandal in which many of his senior officers were fired, and several prominent investors severed their ties with the bank. This new employee had to deal with angry customers and investors from day one. He told me how the issue that happened over five years ago still made him lose sleep at night. He even mentioned that there were days when he would be out visiting with potential customers, only to be treated as a corrupt person and a potential crook —all because of the bank he represented. He was living the *father's sin*. He had done nothing to contribute to this impression other than working for an organization that had a tarnished reputation in the past. He carried this burden everywhere he went.

When I asked him why he hadn't left the bank and moved on to another employer, he replied, "You can change the environment, but you cannot change your internal world; I think it has become so much part of me that I may carry this disgrace for the rest of my life." His life and identity had become so entwined with someone else's mistake that he believed he could never be free of it.

Have you ever felt that way or experienced such an emotion? Have you ever thought you were carrying someone else's shame in such a way that it has become your own, even though you had no part in the original sin?

One of the questions we might ask ourselves is how much did Jephthah's father own his part in this situation? We know that he took in and raised Jephthah, but beyond that, we know little more than his brothers' resentment of him until the day they were grown.

If you are living in the shadow of your *father's sin*, what part does he own, if any? Or does he leave it up to you to find the answer to that question? Do you find the value and worth you were created for in spite of his poor choices? Ultimately, we must all find a solution or reason for our existence in this world if we want to live meaningful lives. If your father refuses to acknowledge his sin or is no longer in your life, you may never find the closure you seek. But that doesn't mean we are cursed to live the life of a social outcast for all our days.

We'll see this as we walk through the life of Jephthah. Life didn't come easy for him, and at times he didn't make the best choices either. There weren't many options for the illegitimate son of a prostitute in that time. Yet, as we'll discover, God used that situation to ensure something good came about at the end.

What changed? What caused such a change to happen? What can we learn from Jephthah's story? As you'll see, there is a great beauty buried under the ashes.

Mother, the other woman: *His mother was a prostitute.* —*Judges 11:1*

Jephthah's mother was not a wife and never was one. She had been labeled a prostitute: A woman with no values. A fringe member of society. An outsider. An outcast. We do not know her complete story. The

Scripture doesn't share what led her to the streets or why she sold her body to men. In truth, it was likely never her Plan A. After all, what little girl grows up dreaming of such a life?

Regardless of her past or future choices, she was nameless, known only by her shame and the fact that she gave birth to a son that was acknowledged and claimed by the father (even though neither of the son or the mother were ever accepted as members of the family). She was not in the limelight, yet she could not be hidden. She was a regrettable choice and a blemish on the family's honor that could not be removed.

What about the son she gave birth to? Yes, what about Jephthah?

Well, he had a mother, and the mother had a son, but there was nothing beyond that. She could never become his father's wife, and Jephthah could never be a legitimate son with a claim to his father's inheritance. They may have had temporary security, but in the eyes of their society, they had no future. The mother's choice and the subsequent consequences gave her a son but deprived her of a whole and abundant life.

Does life ever feel like a give-and-take, bargain kind of thing to you?

Jephthah's mother likely had many men in her life, but she may never have had one she could call her own. She bore him because she was paid for a moment of sinful pleasure by a man who was also guilty of sin. Love wasn't part of the story of Jephthah's life; both parents were joined together for their own gain, one for his physical pleasure and the other for a few coins. He got his share of thrill, and she got her next meal. Their choices set up their son for a life of hardship and loneliness. Their choice also took a toll on their own lives and souls.

In the case of Gilead's home, his selfish act led to a divided house and hostility among the brothers. In the case of Jephthah's mother, her choices led to a life that could never fill the longing and desires of her heart.

Karin was hired as an Au Pair by a couple struggling to balance raising two children and their busy work lives. Karin was a young teenager who wanted to explore the world, and the option of being paid for doing what she loved—caring for children—was a bonus. She took up the job and moved in with this delightful family. Little did she know that the family that looked perfect from the outside was living a separate life of their own. The wife worked with a media company which kept her away most of the day. Her husband worked the graveyard shift and was home most of the day. The constant separation of the husband and wife as well as the added stress of young children led to a sense of alienation between them. All of this made it easy for the man to develop an attraction for the young woman living in his house and caring for his children. She was seen as a person who didn't fight or argue over the money and didn't nag him about completing tasks. She was there to make his life easy and comfortable.

It was an attractive arrangement. Soon things moved to the next level; when the wife was not around, the man started pursuing the young girl. Soon he loved her company more than his wife. Karin, in turn, responded to his advances and began to dream of a future with this man. Eventually, they left his wife's home, taking his children with them.

At first, life together seemed exciting and wonderful. But then Karin began to see what she was missing. She didn't want to stay on the sidelines as a mistress who cared for another woman's children. She wanted to be the woman of the house. She began to press for marriage. Then came the news that they were expecting a child together. Karin was excited about the new baby. But during her pregnancy, she also found out that she didn't have the same love and warmth that she had before for the man she was living with. Karin found him to be too aggressive and demanding, and they often got into arguments and ugly fights over small things. Eventually, the man left Karin alone with their newborn daughter. He returned to the same town as his ex-wife but chose to live with his father rather than return to the first woman he abandoned (if that was ever an option). He rarely called or inquired about Karin or his daughter. Growing up, the little girl would often ask, "why doesn't my father come to pick me up or take me out for a picnic as all other fathers do?" Karin had no answer.

Though young, impressionable, and swept up in the

romance of the moment, Karin became the other woman. She'd gone to bed with a man who wasn't her husband and was cast aside and forgotten once the novelty of their romance had worn off.

What do you do when you have something you deeply love, but it reminds you every day of the pain, hurt, or blunder associated with it? How do you rectify a wrong that was there from the beginning?

It is hard to have an easy answer, but Karin says that, though she loved her daughter, the consequence of her choice meant that she was constantly reminded of her fault and shame. She viewed herself as an outsider, and one who could never truly belong.

In her case, she was taken advantage of. While she wasn't the victim of a violent crime, she was preyed on by an older man who benefited from the situation he was presented with.

Perhaps the grief and sorrow you live under were also caused by someone taking advantage of your innocence or immaturity. Maybe you were given false information that led to making a costly mistake.

If others have used you for their gain, does the shame of being led down a path of trickery ever cause you to feel like you are unworthy to be a member of your family or society?

Does God hold those sins or shames against us?

Brothers of Inheritance: *Gilead's wife also bore him sons, and when they were grown up, they drove Jephthah away. "You are not going to get any inheritance in our family," they said, "because you are the son of another woman." —Judges 11:2*

How does it feel to be part of a group knowing you'll never really belong to it? Perhaps you experienced it during your school days. Maybe you were a part of a team where everyone connected with each other except you. Perhaps you even attend a church where you have been a member for years but still feel invisible.

This sense of alienation was how Jephthah felt all the time while growing up in his home. Though he lived in the same house as the rest of his siblings, he was never considered as one of them. They made sure that he was never made to feel at home in his own home. For them, he was an outsider, and they always saw him as someone who shouldn't be in their house. They looked at him as the "son of another woman'" who had been brought in through trickery and deception. And when it came time to sort out their father's earthly affairs, they had their plan and had already decided the future that didn't include Jephthah or anything that had to do with him.

From the outside, they all lived in the same house, ate the same meals, and perhaps pretended to include him in their activities while their father lived, but in their hearts, he was unacceptable. They didn't see him living with them for long, like a pesky guest who had outstayed his welcome.

How did he feel about all this abuse and harassment that he endured at the hands of his siblings for no fault of his own? Who did he tell about his feelings or what he was going through? On this, Scripture is silent. But anyone who has ever been made to feel unwelcome in their own home—perhaps as a child of divorce and remarriage with new stepsiblings or as the child of an unfavored parent—knows that such a life brings with it pains that cannot be kept bottled up inside forever.

Where do you go when you are made to feel that you do not belong? Why are you constantly belittled and rejected by your kin and in your own home, community, or workplace?

The critical question is, why did the brothers see Jephthah as a threat to them? Why did they treat him like an outsider? What did he do to deserve such treatment from his brothers and to be driven out of his home? Where would he go from here? And where would you go in such a situation? Do you fight or flee?

In verse 2, the brothers are forming a tribe to protect their interests. Whether or not Jephthah was a threat to them makes no difference. How can families turn on one another in this way? What makes one brother plot against another? The short answer is sin and jealousy. The ancient text is filled with such stories: Cain attacked Abel out of anger and jealousy. Joseph's brothers revolted against him because they felt they had been deprived of their father's love and affection. And Jephthah's brothers saw him as an interloper and a shame.

Wealth over relationship

The love for money blinds the hearts of people from seeing the pain in others' eyes (that they often cause). The brothers didn't want Jephthah to have any share in their father's inheritance, so they wanted him out. Customarily, whatever belonged to the father was equally distributed among the siblings. And it is the father who usually decides how to distribute his wealth. But here, the brothers make the call. They wanted more than what rightfully belonged to them, but the only way they could get that was to take someone out of their way, and the easiest target was the "son of the other woman."

Are the brothers just modeling what the father did in the past when he left his wife to go out and made his own choice with a prostitute? He was more concerned about his pleasure than the consequences or how it affected his wife.

When we put wealth or profit over relationships, we, in essence, tell those around us, "I look out for my gain, and I don't care for your pain or what you could lose."

Are there mistakes or *father's sins* repeated by the

children? Possibly. And perhaps the sins of the children are sins of their own making.

When a group decides who is in and who is out based on their own individual benefit, there is always a victim who suffers at the hand of injustice. The decisive majority is most likely not bothered if the other party is left unaccounted, since that only increases their chance of gaining more of the share. These victims don't have the power and are made weak by the greedy few who want more than what rightfully belongs to them.

Have you been driven out, or have you lost your rightful share at the hands of influential people?

Have you ever driven someone out to get what rightfully belonged to them because you viewed them as unworthy or undesirable?

Patrick was an immigrant who traveled to a prosperous country with his family at the age of twelve. After 25 years, he called the new country his second home. He worked hard at various jobs, even as a young boy. First, he helped his dad as a laborer doing home repairs. As he grew up, Patrick picked up various skills that expanded his opportunities. Later he branched out on his own because he couldn't reconcile with his drunk father. Patrick was hardworking and gifted and worked well with his team, mostly made up of his family members. They did well when the housing market peaked, but he could never succeed as most other contractors did.

The main reason was that he was different. Because many of the people he worked alongside didn't have legal work statuses, they were often paid unfair, lower wages. Though he was a legal resident working as a day laborer, he often suffered at the hands of those who viewed him as if he were an undocumented worker.

It wasn't his work or ability that mattered; it was all about where he came from or where he belonged—and how those who could afford to pay refused to do so because they believed they had the advantage. Because he had a family to take care of, he silently suffered at the hands of those privileged companies and people that hired him with the full intention of taking advantage of what they saw as an opportunity to hold onto their wealth.

How often do we ignore the injustice happening

around us because it profits us? How do we contribute to sinful behavior when we are silent about the abuse that happens around us?

Ethical Morality: The Self-righteous Spirit

Jephthah's brothers could not see how a son who didn't come from their mother's womb could claim a piece of the inheritance with them. For them, it was not morally right to associate with such a person from a questionable background.

Who gave them that morality here, or how did they decide what was right or wrong? Was this morality defined to suit their selfish habits? Or was it dictated by their desire to become rich?

Do we justify our morality by using immoral acts? Do we declare ourselves holy so long as those who are "unholy" are put out from among us? How often do we see these same self-righteous acts shown by the brothers play out within our spiritual communities, homes, and groups?

We create our religion when we hurt others with our self-governed faith and practices. When our spirituality excludes others because they are not as "holy" as we are, we push many into the streets.

Questions for Reflection:

a. Have you ever lived through the *father's sin* (see page 21)? Do you feel that you are living the pain and shame caused by the evil and wrongs of others? Can you describe how it feels?

b. How have you judged people because of their *father's sin*?

c. What do you do when something you deeply love reminds you daily of the pain, hurt or blunder associated with it? How do you rectify a wrong that was there from the beginning?

James Levi

2

Fleeing & Settling

So, Jephthah fled from his brothers and settled in the land of Tob, where a gang of scoundrels gathered around him and followed him. —Judges 11:3

When faced with a potential threat to our physical or emotional well-being, we fall into what scientists have dubbed "the fight or flight" response. It's a defense mechanism that God has placed in every human.

You've likely experienced it yourself. Someone raises their voice against you, and you either raise your voice back or retreat emotionally or physically to escape the verbal lashing.

When someone unjustly attacks our character, those around us will often tell us to fight back, to defend ourselves. Sometimes fighting back is the right course of action. But what about the alternative?

When is fleeing the right choice?

Sometimes the only reasonable option left for you is to flee. Just to go away, remove yourself from the people or the situation causing you harm. If you don't, you could very well lose yourself. It can be difficult to cut yourself off from those your life has become entangled with, whether it is the family you are born into, the community you have grown up in, or the people you work with. However, you cannot keep a relationship with those who do not value you or think they are better than you for long before you begin experiencing the physical and emotional fallout of constantly having to be on guard and on the defensive.

This isn't to say you shouldn't have anything to do with those who don't entirely agree with and support your every decision without question. This is in reference to the relationships that define your worth based on a set of circumstances rather than on the intrinsic value that your Creator endowed with you. Perhaps they don't know the one who made you, so they don't know who you are. Thus, they live in ignorance, accepting the opinion of others or the ever-changing whims of society as evidence of their worth.

There are many examples of such fleeing in the sacred text, like at the time when Esau realized he'd been tricked by his younger brother and had lost both his birthright and his father's blessing, his anger burned against Jacob (Genesis 27:41); in response, we see that Jacob followed his mother's instructions and fled. We even see such a fleeing orchestrated by God when King Herod decreed that all the male children (under two years or younger) be killed; Joseph took Mary and the infant Jesus and fled to Egypt (Matthew 2:14).

It is important to flee from closed-mindedness and abusive behaviors because the longer you remain in the company of those who purposefully misunderstand or mistreat you, the more you will be influenced by such thoughts. Those thoughts will, in turn, become accepted "truths" that will weigh on your soul like a heavy chain, preventing you from ever breaking free of the lies and misconceptions that others have buried you under.

It is often said that "hurting people hurt people." In other words, someone living in the bondage of their emotional wounds and the familial sins of the past will be more likely to heap abuse on those around them. This is why you will sometimes see the child of an abusive alcoholic grow up to become an abusive alcoholic. A child who is verbally abused and constantly criticized by their family grows up to be occasionally overly critical of themselves and others in some cases.

Too often, the people who want to hide from their shortcomings and hurts are the ones who are the quickest to point fingers at others and highlight their flaws. Here Jephthah's brothers didn't want to confront the real culprit and sinner, their father, who created the fundamental division in the family. It was easier to turn their wrath on the child, constantly reminded of that sin. It may be easier to take their anger out on the one with no legal claims or protections to the family estate rather than confronting the father and risk losing their inheritance. By declaring Jephthah "the son of another woman" outside of the protected bounds of marriage, they were able to hide behind their self-righteousness as natural-born children and heirs, recognized through the sanctified union of their father and mother's wedding.

In doing so, their father was absolved of his guilt, and Jephthah was made a scapegoat—the one on whom the sin and blame were placed before being driven into the wilderness where it would be vulnerable to hungry predators.

Why do we point the finger at the innocent and pat the back of the real guilty ones? Especially when one is considered an esteemed person and the other is not.

What does it say about us when such things happen in our homes, communities, workplaces, and even on national and global levels?

One of the reasons that we often try to protect the powerful, even when they are in the wrong, is because we hope to benefit in return. Here the children (of a father who was clearly at fault) are now pointing fingers at the one who was not even present at the time of the wrongdoing. It is also evident that they wanted to be on the side of the one who would make them rich and give them a sizable inheritance.

Physical wounds are grievous but often heal faster than emotional scars—especially those received during our earliest years. Recovery from such emotional injuries usually requires a long time of external support and internal strength. In response to such suffering, the spirit can become bitter and hostile, and the natural person you have been created to be somehow gets stunted and lost.

When is it okay to flee? Whenever there is an attempt to devalue who you are in the eyes of the King of Heaven. When the angry voices of those around you threaten to drown out the still voice inside you, that is when running is more important than staying.

When it comes to protecting who you were created to be—by either cutting out those who disparage you or the sinful behaviors that have ensnared or influenced you thus far—fleeing is a courageous act of the spirit.

Unless you run, you will lose yourself.

Sarin was the older of two girls. They lost their father when they were young, and their mother worked hard as a nurse to raise them. While Sarin suffered much in her childhood, it didn't keep her from dreaming of a great life and a future with a peaceful life in a good home and a good neighborhood. She thought those dreams were about to be realized when she married a man named Ebenezer. He was tall and well-built, dark, and handsome looking. The man who wooed her was everything a girl could dream of, but soon after they married, the natural man (that wasn't kind) behind the mask emerged. Ebenezer turned out to be very insecure and took those insecurities out on Sarin, both physically and emotionally. Sarin's dream of a peaceful life and future was shattered. There was no hope. Different people who cared for the couple intervened, trying to reason with Ebenezer, but he had no desire to change his ways. He was a man who was given to passions and pleasures, seeking them wherever he could. When a bout of guilt assailed him, or things didn't go his way, he put the blame solely on Sarin.

It was too much at times. Sarin's hopes for the future were forgotten, and her faith in God and humanity waned a little more each day. Though her family didn't support her abusive husband's actions or behaviors, they felt helpless to do anything because Ebenezer's family was powerful and influential.

A day came when the abuse was too much. Sarin fled from her husband and all the violence that was hurled at her. She knew in her heart that she was more than all she was told and was forced to believe by an insecure man. Still, the trauma of her failed marriage took a toll on her. It took years for her to understand the full effects of those few months of marriage on her mind and spirit. At first, she isolated herself from the world. But then, over the years, she developed a few close friends and became part of a healthy community that prayed with her, cried with her, and helped her heal and stand again.

God didn't forget Sarin. In due time a young man came into her life. He also had a tragic marriage before but was a kindhearted man. He loved and cared for Sarin very much. They got married and eventually had a beautiful daughter who became Sarin's joy and peace. Looking back now, she sees how the emotional words caused by her ex led her to doubt herself and God. She also sees how God can heal and redeem those broken parts of our past. Sarin is living her dream with a godly husband who respects her, loves her, and supports her passion for singing. Every Sunday, he sits with their beautiful daughter in the front row of their church while Sarin sings her heart out to the one who gave her a new spirit and life.

We mustn't allow anyone to take away the beautiful spirit God has deposited in us. Those who have known us the longest or been brought into the most intimate spaces of our lives are often the ones who hurt us the deepest. It is essential to recognize when it is done thoughtlessly and when it is done maliciously. When the acts are continually intentional and malicious, then it is time to flee. Jephthah knew the importance of running from his brothers, who were only after his inheritance. He didn't place worldly wealth or earthly goods over protecting his heavenly spirit and his eternal soul. He knew that protecting the warrior spirit within him was more important than giving in to the temptation of few material possessions. And though it might appear weak to some, he was a strong man who could get up, pack up, and leave without looking back when things weren't right.

God wants us to be mindful of the people we allow to speak into our lives and the reasons behind us giving them such permission.

Can you turn your back and flee when the enemy of your soul begins using the people around you to attack who you are and the spirit that God has given you?

Driving the Warriors from among us: *When they were grown up, they drove Jephthah away.*

One of the powerful weapons we, as humans, use against each other is guilt. When we are legitimately in the wrong, having our guilt revealed to us can lead to godly repentance, but when guilt is used as a tool of shame, often with a religious overtone—it hurts and kills many. Self-righteousness and moral superiority give the perpetrators of such actions a sense of divine right and spiritual authority that empowers them to shame innocent victims and makes them feel as if God is on their side against their victims. In truth, God is never on the side of those who use his name in vain. God never joins hands with the one who abuses his word or his character by harming others.

When religion is sold out, warriors flee.

And that is what happened to Jephthah. The brothers didn't know that one day the inheritance they wanted to claim as their own would be stolen from them because someone more powerful than them would come along and snatch it from their grasp.

They didn't know they needed a man who was a warrior to stand for them, one who could fight for them against the enemy and the injustice inflicted upon them. Without knowledge or care, these brothers of Jephthah drove a warrior from their midst. They cast away their protective shield without knowledge or care, making them vulnerable to the enemy. How often greed blinds us to our defenses and even leads us to destroy the protection needed for our safety.

We see this very well repeated in the life of David, who was a mighty warrior with a God-given ability to fight giants and overcome mighty armies, yet we see Saul got jealous of him and so often tried to kill him. Though Saul's son Jonathan reminded his father about the warrior he was trying to get rid of from their midst, his father didn't heed his son's words.

Jonathan spoke well of David to Saul, his father, and said to him, "Let not the king do wrong to his servant David; he has not wronged you, and what he has done has benefited you greatly." (1 Samuel 19:4)

Even when others try to help us see the bigger picture, we are so blinded, like Saul, that we bring our downfall through our actions that undermine us.

Have we driven the warriors from among us —those gifted and talented ones who were for us—because we thought they were against us or taking away our share? Are we working against ourselves and being blinded to the dangers lurking around us because of our greed?

Often the people we drive away are the ones we need the most in the future. It's not what the brothers thought could save them (the inheritance) that truly saved them, but the one who they thought was unholy (Jephthah). The brother they rejected was the one who became their savior. The people of Israel would go on to reject another brother in the same way. Of Christ, Scripture says, "He came to that which was his own, but his own did not receive him" (John 1:11).

How often do we see this rejection play out in Scripture? How often do we see it play out in life? There are three reasons we reject the warrior among us, and each serves as a mark against us rather than a mark against them.

1. We like to be self-dependent

The brothers of Jephthah thought they would be better off, so they drove him off, and he found his place among others who recognized his strength and talents (Judges 11:3). We rarely feel the need for a savior until we hit rock bottom. Most of us want to believe that we will be okay on our own or act as if everything is fine. We'll put on a show for others that portrays us as vital and in control when we know that even the breath, we have is a gift and we do not have any power to extend even a minute to our lives. And so, we miss out on the ones God has placed in our lives to serve as a helper and co-defender, leaving us vulnerable to future attacks.

2. The saviors God sends us don't fit our mold

As a society, we have a significant attraction to superheroes. In any given year, you're bound to see ads for a hero franchise's newest chapter. Even though we know that heroes with superhuman strength and ability don't exist, we gravitate toward their stories, dress up in their costumes, and we long for a world where there are heroes like these to battle against the evils in our world.

Our hearts were designed to seek out a Savior. But when we hear of God becoming one among us, living a life of homelessness and poverty while simultaneously calling us to follow Him to live by a higher standard, we become disturbed, perturbed, and afraid. When we are shown examples of the saviors God sends to aid his people, it confuses us because they don't fit the typical bill or satisfy our superman image and desire.

The fallen world doesn't want God to become a man but wants us humans to become gods ourselves. It encourages us to follow our misguided hearts, live as we see fit, and become the heroes of our own stories. In the process, it conditions us to ignore the one who stepped out of heaven, taking up the flesh and blood of humans, to die a barbaric and unjustified death so that we could be saved from ourselves. The world does not accept the one who died on the cross and rejects any who stand in his name.

Jephthah's story parallels and foreshadows what God intended to do for humanity through his Son, Jesus Christ. He was one among the Jewish people, His coming was prophesied centuries before His birth, and just as Jephthah was rejected by his brothers, Christ was abandoned by His own because He didn't fit the mold of who they thought the Messiah ought to be. They drove Him away out of jealousy and spite, though He was the one they had been waiting to come and save them.

3. Grace seems too simple

When God extends His grace, it looks too simple for some; the question often asked is how could His only expectation of us be to acknowledge our failings and accept His gift of salvation? Therefore, like Naaman, the commander of the king of Aram's army (2 Kings 5), we don't take the word of God spoken by His prophets earnestly because it seems too simple, nor do we pay him any mind.

When we think of grace, we tend to think of its most basic definition, "favor" or "approval." But Merriam-Webster shows us the word has a far deeper and more costly meaning. Grace is "the unmerited divine assistance given to humans for their regeneration or sanctification." It's also defined as an act of clemency or full pardon.

Someone giving up his life and dying for every person ever to live and breathe is not an easy concept to accept. Unless we know our true worth in the eyes of the Savior, we will miss the truth behind grace. Grace is what gives our lives value, and grace is what makes us worthy of being redeemed.

At the same time, self-doubt prevents us from accepting God's Grace. We live in a world that tries to put a hefty price tag on everything perceived to have value, so we also try to gain our salvation through our efforts. In turn, the value (or lack thereof) that we place on God's Grace plays out in how we extend grace to those around us. Jephthah's brothers had no regard for their brother and, by extension, showed their lack of respect toward their Heavenly Father, who had graced them with the very riches they sought to hoard for themselves.

Questions for Reflection:

a. When is it okay to flee? Have you ever found yourself in a place or situation where it was challenging to escape even though you knew it was the best thing to do? Please share your experience.

b. Do we point the finger at the innocent and pat the back of the real guilty ones? (Especially when one is considered an esteemed person and the other is not). What does it say about us when such things happen in our homes, communities, workplaces, and even on national and global levels?

3

Lost in the Living

So, Jephthah fled from his brothers and settled in the land of Tob, where a gang of scoundrels gathered around him and followed him. —Judges 11:3

A warrior is born to fight battles.

They live to save people and bring deliverance.

But as we follow along the story of Jephthah, we see that he is now made to settle for less than who he is. He doesn't fight any battles worth mentioning. There is no attack he must counter to protect those around him. Have you ever lived in a wretched place, cut off from everything you thought your life would be one day? And believing that perhaps you weren't destined for the great things you'd grown up dreaming of achieving. What compromises have you made to survive from one day to the next? What ideas or behaviors have you embraced that you might have rejected and taken a different path to that point?

Though we might convince ourselves that such a life protects us and provides for us in some way, for the time being, the truth is it doesn't help us become who we are meant to be. It doesn't fulfill our purpose, and it doesn't develop our true identity. While we may have ended up in this place to escape those attempting to kill us or those who have grievously abused us, if we stay here for long, we may forget who we are. And *whose* we are.

That's what happened to Moses, the mighty leader who, roaming around in the wilderness with his father-in-law's sheep, gave the excuse that he didn't know how to speak well—an essential qualification for a deliverer (according to him). He was running away from Egypt, where his people had rejected him, and his temper and passion had made him a murderer. In his youth, he considered himself a warrior, a hero. Then when he started walking up and down those hills, following the sheep, he may have thought he'd made a mistake, or perhaps was himself a mistake. He concluded in his heart that he had nothing to do with the deliverance mission or such projects anymore. He didn't feel right leading the same people who had rejected him.

Jephthah may have felt the same struggle because of what had happened to him; he perhaps thought Tob, and a life of crime was his final destination. Maybe this was all there was for him, or he was meant and made to be —the leader of a band of scoundrels.

Sometimes the path to our destiny involves some humbling experiences. We find ourselves suddenly unemployed through no fault of our own, through layoffs, mismanagement, and company closures, and we are forced to take on a job that society would label as "beneath us." Or a person we thought we could trust turns out to be untrustworthy and we are left "tainted" and "shamed" or even "soiled." And so, we retreat and hide away because we cannot bear to be seen, pitied, or mocked by those around us.

After being anointed the future King of Israel, David was brought into King Saul's palace, where he enjoyed every luxury a shepherd boy could dream of. But then we see David had to face a threat to his life. He had to flee, hide in caves, and constantly wander about to stay one step ahead of the king's murderous wrath. Yet it was during that time that some of the most potent psalms we still turn to today were written.

Knowing that the place we flee during seasons of distress is not our ultimate destination is essential for fulfilling our purpose. It prevents us from becoming too settled into our hideaway, where we can be pulled further away from the work God has prepared for us and the future that He promises us.

It seems Jephthah knew deep down in his heart that he was meant to be more than just hanging out with a few scoundrels until he came to an unsavory end. Within every fiber of his being, he knew beyond every doubt that he was born to fight some big fight and to win great victories for God and his people, and he never wanted to see that door close on him. It is essential to know that many warriors get wounded in training and battle, but that should not make one give up on a warrior's real purpose. The process of stepping away and finding a place like Tob can be, for the time being, a healing place, a comforting thing—but in the long run, it can become a depressing place if we do not follow the warrior spirit within us. Eventually, the call will come for us to return home and to our rightful place, our true calling (where we find our identity and purpose). Heeding that call may not be easy. It wasn't easy for Jephthah either.

The Scoundrels

We don't know who found who, but Judges 11:3 says that a band of "scoundrels" started following Jephthah—making him their leader. Even though he was not one among them, his true home was not among them, and his family didn't belong to the people following him. We're given the impression that he fully embraced his role and rose to become a force to be reckoned with.

Why did he attach himself to such disreputable

people? Jephthah was a warrior; his work did not belong among such a community, but he was willing to accept and be counted as one of them. A few things seem to distinguish Jephthah as we consider this brief statement about his life with the scoundrels.

He didn't differentiate people based on who they were.

As a victim of discrimination himself, the hurt caused by his family allowed him to extend a hand of grace to others who found themselves on the outskirts of society either by choice or by being driven away from their own families, just as he had been. We also see the hint of mercy he was willing to show others, the compassion he'd been denied in his home. Instead of acting toward these misfits, rebels, and rascals the way he'd been treated, he shows them the consideration and care he'd wanted his brothers to show him. As the leader, it would have been his responsibility to resolve the conflicts between his men, to provide rewards and discipline, and to give orders for when and how to act. He would have devised strategies and learned to take the counsel of those with experience outside his own. And it would have been his responsibility to ensure each of his men returned home and were presented with their deserved portion.

What do we do with our pain? How do we respond to those who have hurt us? Do we inflict that same pain on others, or do we treat them with the grace and mercy we wish we'd been treated with? It could have been easier for Jephthah to hurt others the way he'd been. As the head of a band of scoundrels, he could have quickly marched against his brothers and taken what was his. Instead, he chose a path that would prepare him for the showdown with his brothers later on.

He built relationships rather than isolating himself.

Jephthah sought and connected with people when he would have been justified in cutting himself off from the world. Rather than retreating into himself, he joined with others who may have been treated even worse than he had been. He understood the importance of being surrounded by others seeking to better their lives in some way. He might have known they weren't the "best people" to hang out with, yet these people, too, deserved to be treated with dignity and respect.

Jephthah displays an outstanding quality of a leader in that, even being in a strange place or an area where he didn't belong, he built a community that would go on to make all the difference between victory and defeat for the people who'd rejected him.

Jephthah was willing to learn, gain, and find something new and of value, even when everything he had before was lost. The people around him were not the best of the best, yet he knew everyone could contribute and teach him something and that he could contribute in return. He gave himself entirely to his role, and if the elders from his homeland had not thought about him and had not come looking for him to take him back, he likely would have remained with the scoundrels all his life. The ability to fully commit to a cause, regardless of past hurts, is a profound quality for a leader and warrior. Rather than choosing to be forever the victim of an unfair past, he decided to step up and out in an unfamiliar environment, which in turn equipped him with the skills necessary to become the savior his people would one day need.

Mohamed was a very gifted musician and a well-liked man. He learned to play various instruments, and he was good at them. He opened a small shop near his hometown of Ankara, Turkey and taught music to interested students. Though the villagers weren't prosperous, he had a good business that kept him going. His wife was also a teacher who taught in a school nearby, and many of her students came to Mohamed's music class in the evenings. Everything was going well until one day; they discovered that the school would open a music department of its own and was hiring a music teacher.

Mohamed knew that the new music department would impact his business, and he could lose all his students, as they could now obtain free lessons at school. This disturbed Mohamed, and he lost many nights of sleep over it. He tried to talk to his wife, though she understood, she couldn't soothe his worry. Eventually, she suggested that he apply to become a music teacher; that way, he could still have the students and earn enough money to cover the shortfall caused by the decreased income of private music lessons.

Though wisdom was in his wife's advice, he couldn't understand how she could be insensitive to him. In his pain, he used harsh words at his wife, telling her that she could not see how his lifelong dream and business were getting destroyed. His powerful words put them at odds with each other, and they kept to themselves for several days.

Then one day, he came to her and asked forgiveness, saying that he was sorry for hurting her with his words, but he also said that he felt that she didn't see his pain and his hurt, and the only way he could show it to her was to hurt her with words so that she would feel as he felt.

Mohamed chose to be so caught up in his hurts that he refused to see his wife as an ally. Instead, he decided to view her as the enemy and, like Jephthah's brothers, poured his hurt and anger about a situation beyond his wife's control out on her, driving her away. Even his show of apology was merely a justification for his wrong actions. Instead of being governed by mercy and grace and looking at the opportunities presented to him by this new challenge, Mohamed chose the easier path of self-centered anger.

How do we respond to the challenges and the upheavals we face in our lives? Do we act like the brothers and vent our anger on those around us, justified or not? Or do we follow the more challenging path that allows us to be wronged, to be forced to begin again, and to embrace the challenges presented to us, trusting that God sees and redeems the wrongs committed against us?

Jephthah had the opportunity to make others around him feel the pain he was going through, but he chose not to be like those who had wronged him. He decided to be different, so he became a mighty warrior.

Questions for Reflection:

a. Have you ever been driven to a place, cut off from everything you thought your life would be one day? (and believing that perhaps you weren't destined for the great things you'd grown up dreaming of achieving). What compromises have you made to survive from one day to the next? What ideas or behaviors have you embraced or rejected in that place?

b. What do we do with our pain? How do we respond to those who have hurt us?

c. Do we inflict that same pain on others or treat them with the grace and mercy we wish we'd been treated with?

d. How do we respond to the challenges and the upheavals we face in our lives? Do we vent our anger on those around us, justified or not? Where do you see God in it?

4

Calling

Sometime later, when the Ammonites were fighting against Israel, the elders of Gilead went to get Jephthah from the land of Tob. "Come," they said, "be our commander, so we can fight the Ammonites." Jephthah said to them, "Didn't you hate me and drive me from my father's house? Why do you come to me now when you're in trouble?" The elders of Gilead said to him, "Nevertheless, we are turning to you now; come with us to fight the Ammonites, and you will be head over all of us who live in Gilead."—Judges 11:4–8

It is common for people to associate one's home with their taste, lifestyle, and even outlook. A person living in a gated community is often perceived as affluent and someone to aspire to be like, very unlikely on the wrong side of the track, as they say. Likewise, the stage of life you find yourself in can also say much about who you are. A school-aged child is seen as still immature and needing guidance. A recent college graduate is viewed as someone who has their entire life spread about before them. And the lonely, older man who spends his days raising his fist at the kids daring to set foot on his lawn is perceived as one who never learned the value of kindness or compassion.

But sometimes, our place is deceptive, not just to others but to ourselves. It can confuse and give a very different picture of who you are and your purpose. Without direction and purpose, people can get lost in their surroundings and circumstances and be forgotten by those who once knew them, disappearing into the mists of time.

Consider those unfortunate souls whose bodies litter the slopes of Mount Everest. At one point, they were sons and daughters, husbands and wives, business leaders, and world-renowned travelers. Today, many are known simply by the monikers given to them by others attempting the treacherous climb—their names unknown or forgotten in time.

The truth is who you are created to be is not lost with time, distance, or experience. Certainly not in the eyes of the Lord. Knowing that helps us to recognize our call more clearly when we feel unseen, unheard, and unwanted by those who should have cared, supported, or come alongside us. The pain you feel in your exile is real—the hurts you experienced at the hands of those who should have nurtured you cannot be denied. But what the apostle Paul wrote is still pertinent: absolute joy and contentment can still be found even amid your suffering (Philippians 2:12–13).

Living Outside of the Promise

After being driven away by his brothers, Jephthah lived far from his people. It had been a while since he had seen them or was seen with them. He had escaped and was now well settled in a place called Tob. But deep down, Jephthah knew who he was—a warrior—and warriors are known for the battles they fight. But in Tob, he wasn't fighting any war or advancing the cause of justice. He was passing his time wandering around with a gang, doing whatever it took to survive.

Though some will say their identity and family are found among the gang members they hang out with, gangs are for those who want to see some excitement and pleasure or for those who are lost and don't have a purpose.

True warriors smell the battles worth joining and long to fight and win them. It is in these fights that the future of others beyond oneself is decided. And the cost of these battles is nothing short of utter self-sacrifice. These battles are not entered for self-gratitude or personal achievement but to make a difference in the lives of others.

This is where your gift meets with your purpose in life. Here is where your identity is defined. You feel deep within you that this is what you were born to do.

Jephthah may have been labeled a scoundrel while in Tob, but that label was far from being his identity. And while Jephthah himself may have been confused and might have begun to embrace the title others had given him, a time was coming when his true identity would be made clear. In the same way, you may be in a place where you have been mislabeled and have felt set aside by those in your life, or it may even seem that God did it. Your story is still ongoing. Your moment of clarity, renewed identity, and purpose may be closer than you think.

One day can change everything. A burning bush can bring the lost vision back. An answered prayer can revive a dead dream.

One day, Jephthah saw some people approaching. They looked familiar, like people he'd known in the past. Many resembled him, likely bringing back many painful memories of his rejection, agony, and loss. At that moment, staying in Tob might have seemed more straightforward than picking up his belongings and pitching his tent among his brothers. And yet, that's precisely what God was calling him to do.

Ron grew up in an unstable home that left him rudderless for a time after growing up. I met Ron at a time in his life when everything was taking a new shape and beginning to look brighter. Though he was confined to a cell in prison, there was a different spirit within him because he had connected with the purpose of his life.

Born and raised in a family that constantly moved to where temporary construction workers were needed meant there was very little stability for Ron or the rest of his siblings. When the work dried up, a new call was received, and the family packed up their old van and headed to a new town. It didn't matter if it was in the middle of the school year or if it meant severing what connections they'd managed to build in the time they'd lived in that town. This transient life didn't just rob young Ron of friends and community; it kept him from finding his true purpose and passion. But now, inside the prison, he was settled and was well-accepted as a chef who could create delicious dishes from nothing.

Fellow inmates had seen his magical ability to make dishes and desserts that could shame even the experts in his field. But how did such a transformation happen to a person who had lost everything as a young man, and had been arrested often, and who was now incarcerated for his past wrongs? Ron shared with me that, though he knew he was born to create in the kitchen, he spent his youth running after the wrong things because he got distracted by the allure of belonging with a group of others who felt just as disconnected from the world as he did.

Ron explained that growing up, the only thing that seemed to anchor him was the few friends he'd made who most parents would call "bad influences." Soon he found himself engaged in dealing drugs. This involved other criminal acts, which made him run from the law. Vulnerable and often left to his own devices, Ron was the perfect mark for predators looking to lure unwary boys into their dens and put out into the shady alleys and darkly lit clubs to bring back the dealer's illegal gains. Although he joined the gang, hoping to find an identity and a steadfast community, he knew very well that he was not supposed to be doing the things he was doing. Every night when he would go to sleep, he would wonder if this was all his life was meant to be. This question kept coming to him every night, and he didn't know how to answer it. By the time he was arrested and sent to prison, he was a depressed and angry young man.

But then, one day, they needed some help in the kitchen, and somebody came looking for him. That day changed everything for Ron. Even though he was cooking for prisoners instead of wealthy customers, his location didn't stop him from connecting with his spirit and feeling what he was called to do in life. For the first time, others saw in him something that he had been created for, and they soon gave him a permanent position in the prison kitchens. From then on, there was no turning back. He has been handling the entire unit kitchen by himself for over a decade and has trained hundreds of other inmates, helping them find their gifts and purpose.

Ron will be released soon on parole, and he already has a few excellent restaurants waiting for him to come and work with them. He dreams of one day starting his own restaurant and employing people like him who missed their first chance to become who they were created to be. He understands what it means to live in a temporary place, thinking your circumstances are fixed and that you are destined to leave your true calling unclaimed and unfulfilled.

God never forgets us, whether we're locked in a prison or hiding in a place called Tob. Eventually, He sends people to look for us and bring us back to our inheritance—the center of his will. Scripture says that God never wants anyone to perish, so He sent His Son to deliver us from our shame and brokenness (2 Peter 3:9). The question we must ask ourselves is, do we trust the one who comes calling us?

Recognizing the call: *"Come," they said, "be our commander so that we can fight the Ammonites." —Judges 11:6*

When the enemy came threatening his family's lives, and the battle arose, they came looking for Jephthah. People can ignore you but cannot overlook your gifts when their survival depends on your skills. So long as there was no battle to be waged, nobody cared about or was bothered by what was happening with Jephthah. The brothers and the community thought they could live without Jephthah, but the day the war came close to their neighborhood and into their backyard, there was no other choice than to look for him.

Why do people ignore you but want your gifts? Why do people forget you in peacetime but in wartime, they cry out for you?

We see two things here: a. Your life's calling is more significant than the situation you are in, and knowing your gift helps you recognize your calling. b. Sometimes a battle cry helps us connect with our true calling. Peacetime may give us comfort where we are, but wartime allows us (and those around us) to see exactly what we are made of. Just because they can live without you in peacetime doesn't mean they can ignore you for long because their lives may depend on you when the battle rages.

Let's see our gifts as something we can use to serve and save others. Can we understand that we are made for the benefit of others and not just for ourselves? It is time to stop living alone and begin living with others in mind. The strange thing is, we are called to love those who have hurt us and ignored us just as much as those who have blessed us (Matthew 5:43–48). "But such a thing is unthinkable," you say. "You don't know what I have suffered at their hands!"

Consider this: Jephthah was born to save the same people who had driven him out. The people who never stood with him were the ones who pleaded with him to stand with them in their hour of need. At that moment, they recognized that even before the battle was fought, Jephthah was called to be made their head and chief.

During peacetime, people may not see your strengths, but at the first sign of trouble, their eyes are opened, and they finally see you for who you are. Or they may see it, but fear or jealousy prevents them from saying it out loud.

Perhaps you, like Joseph, recognize God's calling in your life early on. That means you should refrain from involving yourself in an unnecessary fight for others to recognize you. Instead, have patience. Wait for the Lord to choose when He elevates you to your position. Have faith that the right people will come looking for you at the right time.

Jephthah could have fought his brothers in the beginning and could have forced them to recognize him as their leader, but he didn't try to snatch what was his before it was meant to be his.

We must wait for God's battle and let others come to us in his time. Some situations arise or happen in the lives of others so that our calling might be clarified and recognized, allowing us to connect to our true gifts, like when the king of Egypt had a disturbing dream and couldn't sleep. This disturbance led his cupbearer to remember the young Hebrew boy he'd left forgotten in prison. That boy's gift, which had foretold the cupbearer's return to favor, was used to prepare an entire nation for an unprecedented famine.

Don't give up on your calling just because it seems your calling is getting late in coming. What seems like a delay to you may be the Lord laying the groundwork for your debut.

Sometimes God shakes things up and does the unexpected so that we give up living in Tob and move onto our true calling. It happened with Moses. He had left his people and his surroundings to escape the threat to his life, but then God needed a deliverer and found one in Moses. Had Moses not recognized the call, he would have lived the rest of his days in the deserts of Midian, living and dying unrecognized by those he'd been called to. The question we need to ask today is: Are we able to see the bushes that are burning right in our neighborhood? Will we be courageous enough to stop and take off our sandals and walk towards it?

Had Jephthah not recognized the call behind his people's plea, he too would have passed from this world as a forgotten soul who spent his days as a wanderer. A man without a country and a home.

What do you do when the ones who have hurt you most seek you out to help them in their distress? Do you leave them as they left you to suffer, or do you look beyond their words and see the Call of your Creator in your life?

Yielding to the Call: *Jephthah said to them, "Didn't you hate me and drive me from my father's house? Why do you come to me now when you're in trouble?"—Judges 11:7*

Why is it important to yield to a call and sometimes others' trouble? Isn't it wiser to mind our own business and not get trapped in other's affairs? We need to understand that our call is often tied in with others' business; rarely, it is found in our needs.

The more we yield to others' pain, the more we connect to our true selves and find our calling fulfilled.

The more we isolate ourselves from others' troubles, the less we will know our purpose. We can see this practically in how life takes its course. No one can birth a child unless she carries a baby for almost nine months and the ensuing labor pains. It is in the process of giving birth that she becomes a mother.

How a mother attaches herself to the child growing inside her, the one she has never seen or known, is miraculous. She has no idea who the baby will be or what they will accomplish, yet when the labor pains begin, she finds a deep strength within herself that enables her to bring that child into the world.

The moment the baby is conceived, she becomes a different person. Once the baby is born, the mother may or may not be part of its life, but her gift of being a mother is realized the moment she chooses to love and protect that child's life as her own.

Likewise, Jephthah was a warrior and may have fought the battle here and there, but the actual confirmation of his calling happened on the *battlefield*. Therefore, it was important for Jephthah to yield to the painful moment of submitting to the people who had rejected him—going and participating in the trouble of those who had caused trouble for him. This moment was a more significant battle for Jephthah than any he would fight on the field. There he knew what he could do, and he did well, but when he had to face the battle of his own heart, his past hurt, and his pain of rejection, he could only ask: Why now? What's changed?

It is essential to know that our gifts will go wasted, and our talents can go unrecognized if we refuse to allow ourselves to move past our hurts. Here Jephthah had been hurt badly and was dealing with his past pain. He could have ignored his people in their trouble, but that would have meant he would never experience a fullness of purpose. He had to move beyond his hurt, pain, and rejection before he could rescue others from theirs.

To accept what his brothers (the ones who had wounded him) have finally accepted (him to be their leader) is a tough thing to do because that almost means to agree with them or to be on the same side (of your oppressor, which you don't ever want it to happen. Because the wound is still not healed).

How ironic that our gifts and destiny are tied to moving past our hurts and pain by forgiving the people who have wounded us.

Once we have made peace with ourselves—accepting that God can and will use our pain and even abuse to strengthen us and equip us to step into our call—we cannot hold on to that anger and grief any longer. We also recognize that holding on to it is toxic, not just to us but even to those around us. God is interested in our freedom, in our peace, as much as in us finding our purpose. He wants to give us rest from past hurts and thus invites us to trust Him.

The longer Jephthah lived in Tob, the place of his refuge and away from his abusers, the farther he was from connecting with his warrior spirit. He couldn't become who he was meant to be without accepting people for who they were. He had to recognize his abusers as broken people themselves and the ones who—to their chagrin—would help him step into the role God had ordained would be his from the beginning.

Stepping into the Call: *Jephthah answered, "Suppose you take me back to fight the Ammonites and the Lord gives them to me— will I really be your head?" —Judges 11:9*

This is when you decide to step up to your call rather than press further into your hurt. Here you choose to move and connect to your future and let go of your past and pain. The moment you do, you realize that living a life of purpose is more significant than remaining angry over all the rejection. While you do not necessarily forget everything that happened, you extend forgiveness by remembering God's forgiveness and promises to you.

You don't fight the people who hurt you but instead choose to believe they have played a role in shaping you and bringing you to a place where you will fight the more significant battle—the fight they couldn't fight for themselves. This is the path Joseph took with his brothers who couldn't bring themselves to accept the blame for their past actions (Genesis 50:20), and it is the path Jesus took when our sins nailed him to the cross (Luke 23:34).

We can only step into our destiny if we learn to recognize our real battle and where our focus and energy should be. Paul reveals this to us in Ephesians 6:10–17, even going so far as to use the language of battle when he declares that our war is not against "flesh and blood" but against "the spiritual forces of evil in the heavenly realms" (v. 12).

When we recognize who the true enemy is and arm ourselves appropriately, who we are and what we are called to is fully realized when we enter the battle.

Jephthah did that. He realized that he didn't have to fight his brothers anymore, though they were the ones who had driven him out. They robbed him of a decent childhood and were the cause of him living a life away from his home and running around with the scoundrels. He understood all those events were painful and hard for him, but to connect with who he was as a warrior, he had to win the battle within him and step into that call of forgiveness that God had first set before him.

Are you willing to let go of those hurts and pains that have impacted your life? Will you be able to show kindness to the ones who have abused you, taken away your childhood, and made you a wanderer?

You can when you accept God's call that invites you to revisit your place of pain with him at your side.

Visiting Your Place of Pain: *Jephthah went with the elders of Gilead, and the people made him head and commander over them. And he repeated all his words before the Lord in Mizpah.* —*Judges 11:11*

It must have been challenging to take the elders at their word. Still, Jephthah trusted them; he gave them a second chance. He purposely agreed with their request and cast his lot in with theirs, intertwining their lives together once more.

It is not easy to return to a place where you've been driven out or abused. Visiting those places can bring back old memories, but it can also become a place of healing. Unless we experience healing, we will not be effective in our purpose. There is no shortcut, no road that leads us around the hurt; we must allow God to walk us through it.

The journey through the *valley of the shadow of the death* that is our past pain gives us internal stability and strength that keeps us facing the real battles we were made to fight.

What happens when we go through that place of our past hurt assures us of certain important truths:

1. It tells us that pain and hurt cannot destroy us if we trust God and believe in his promises.

2. It also says that we are stronger than we think because those hurts tried to make us look weak and hopeless.

3. It serves as an example for others to never give up and becomes a warning to the abusers that they will not ultimately be successful in their plans.

4. The purpose of God is bigger than the pain of abuse.

Jephthah was made the head of the same people who had driven him away. He returned to the place from which he had fled for his life. Not only was he back in his home, but now he was made the head. This promotion wouldn't have happened without him coming to the same place that once filled him with fear.

What is your fear of the past? What is the future that God wants to raise out of the place of your fear?

The site of our past fears can become the place of our futures, but that can only happen if we learn to recognize and step into the identities God has given us and use that strength to face the fears that tried to rob us of all we are promised. The example of Jephthah is that the warrior doesn't fight just any battle, the warrior fights for the redemption and the future of his people, and in the process, God takes us to our inner healing and victory.

Questions for Reflection:

a. Do you feel that people sometimes ignore you but want your gifts? Do you also think that people forget you in their good times but come to you in their difficulty? Why? How does it make you feel?

b. What do you do when people who have hurt you seek you out to help them in their distress? Do you leave them as they left you to suffer, or do you look beyond their words and see the Call of your Creator in your life?

c. What is your fear of the past? What is the future that God wants you to have from the place of your fear?

d. Have you ever been in a place where you felt that you were fighting a losing battle with someone who has no desire to see reason or truth? What do you do then?

5

Just Fight

Then Jephthah sent messengers to the Ammonite king with the question: "What do you have against me that you have attacked my country? —
Judges 11:12

There's a difference between bullies and warriors. A bully roams about, looking for fights where none exist. A warrior doesn't go into battle without having a real reason.

When the elders of Gilead came to Jephthah, they asked him to jump into a fight with the Ammonites, but Jephthah showed wisdom and restraint. Rather than rushing to battle filled with visions of glory and honor, we read that he "sent a messenger to the Ammonite king with the question: "What do you have against me?" (v. 12).

As the new head of the people of Gilead, Jephthah recognized that if the Ammonites had a claim against Gilead, they had a claim against him. As the leader, it was his responsibility first to seek peace and, if necessary, right any insults or wrongs committed by his people against the Ammonites and their king before proceeding to war.

King Solomon wrote, "Wisdom is better than great strength" (Ecclesiastes 9:16). We see that Jephthah had both. He had the wisdom to seek out the root of the problem and the strength to practice restraint rather than rushing into action without considering the long-term ramifications.

A well-known phrase is often given to parents of young children: choose your battles. Having the opportunity to fight isn't enough reason to get involved in the conflict, especially if you're being brought into the fight by someone who is already directly involved.

Wisdom knows when to restrain and when to move forward. Here, Jephthah exhibits one of the most outstanding qualities of a warrior, trying to understand what has brought the nations to this point. When confronted with conflict and a potential battle, wise leaders need the following characteristics:

Have a clear understanding of the conflict.

Don't rely on hearsay; instead, go straight to the source so they can explain their side of the argument. Jephthah did this by sending a messenger to the Ammonite king, allowing his potential enemy to explain himself (v. 12).

Respect the opponent as a person and educate themselves on their opponent's grievances and perspective. Jephthah asks the king for a reason behind his action. He wants to create a space where others can explain themselves, so he can understand them, what shapes their thinking and, ultimately, their behavior. He listened to the king's claim that Israel came out of Egypt and stole the land "from the Arnon to the Jabbok, all the way to the Jordan" (v. 13) and his demand for the immediate return of all the land claimed in the grievance.

Rather than responding in the heat of the moment, Jephthah looked at the facts and came to his understanding based on the truth.

Have courage in confronting any falsehood with the truth. Jephthah challenged the idea behind the aggression because he knew every battle is fought based on specific beliefs or concepts that may or may not be found in the truth. He firmly and respectfully took the Ammonite king back to school with a history lesson (v. 14–21), reminding him that it was their king who rejected Israel's request to pass peacefully through the land to their place and instead "mustered all his troops and encamped at Jahaz and fought with Israel" (v. 21). The former king came against Israel in the name of his God and Israel defended itself with the strength of the God of Israel. And the God of Israel won the victory and took the land, giving it to his people.

Appeal for peace. When we are in the wrong, we should be the first to admit it when it's brought to our attention.

However, when conflict results from a misunderstanding, a perceived slight, or is being unfairly directed at you, you are within your right to defend yourself to restore peace. In his reply, Jephthah pointed out that the king's grievance wasn't with Israel but with his God, Chemosh, who failed to bring them victory over Israel hundreds of years before. Furthermore, no other king from that time forward had quarreled with Israel...until now (v. 23–26).

Always uphold justice. Jephthah ends his rebuttal to the Ammonite king, declaring that Amon is in the wrong, not Israel or Gilead, and appeals to "the Lord, the Judge" to judge between the two nations (v. 27).

Jephthah knew fighting was not his only purpose; he was restoring peace between two nations who had been living side by side—if not peacefully, at least not aggressively—for centuries. He recognized the preciousness of life, and the devastation that would follow should the nations go to war. Therefore, he sought to keep himself and others from making a wrong move based on inaccurate information. He was willing to respect people who showed him no respect—both among his people and the Ammonites. In doing so, he attempted to forge peace and friendship through mutual respect and understanding, hoping that his actions would encourage his enemies to do the same.

Know Your Enemy

Many of us do not win the battles in our lives because we do not understand who our enemy is or why our enemy is waging the fight in the first place. Understanding your opponent and why they are against you is more important than beating them. This applies to all other conflicts that happen in us and around us. It applies to how we approach the disputes arising in our marriages and in complicated family problems that threaten to separate its members. It encourages us to take time to understand our teenager's struggles before judging and correcting them and to understand a colleague's resentments before destroying a friendship or work relationship.

Kevin's parents struggled to communicate with their teenage Son. Everything they tried to teach him seemed to go in one ear and out the other. To them, it appeared that Kevin had no care for the future. Instead, he was more interested in video games and parties.

Kevin often stayed up late after school, glued to the flashing screen. On weekends, he would hardly be found at home. His teachers had frequent concerns regarding his failing grades and inattentiveness. None of their interventions or meetings with school counselors seemed to make a difference. The issue escalated to Kevin's father's refusal to be in the same room with his son. He was angry and frustrated at how his son had turned out to be.

To add to their trouble, Kevin moved out and started living with a woman who was much older than him. The father commented, "I don't understand where all the morals that we taught him have gone."

The more Kevin rebelled, the more his dad got frustrated and separated. There was no place for any connection. There was no place for open and honest communication. And therefore, there was no chance for reconciliation.

What do you do when you're fighting a losing battle with someone who has no desire to see reason or truth?

Do you continue to engage with them, fighting the same hopeless battle repeatedly?

Where most people give up and surrender to the enemy or set out with the goal of burying their adversary, Jephthah showed his strength in restraining himself from violence, seeking instead to know his enemy honestly. At the same time, he was trying to work out a better plan and see if there was any room for negotiation, a way by which this misunderstanding could be corrected or rectified for the greater good of all parties involved.

Know Your History: *"Then the Lord, the God of Israel, gave Sihon and his whole army into Israel's hands, and they defeated them. Israel took over all the land of the Amorites who lived in that country, capturing all of it from the Arnon to the Jabbok and from the desert to the Jordan."*

Once a person accepts a lie as the truth, then for them, it becomes the truth no matter what others say or believe. Right or wrong, once someone thinks they are morally correct, then anyone else not living in compliance with that belief is morally wrong. When both parties are firmly entrenched in the idea that they are morally in the right and the "other" is purely in the wrong, it is virtually impossible to resolve a conflict; we see this unfold in disputes over politics every day.

Jephthah listened to the enemy, gave them time to explain, and tried to understand the rationale behind the Ammonites' aggression. But then, after verifying the facts, he understood that the Ammonites believed a lie, there was no truth in their complaint or claims, and yet they were fully committed to their belief.

The only way he could know what they thought was a lie was because he knew his history well. Knowing who you are and where you have come from is important because this knowledge will keep you safe and focused on where you want to go. Jephthah knew that Israel was not the aggressor, nor were they thieves. Why? Because someone in his life had obeyed one of God's commands to teach the younger generations the stories of their past so that they would a) recognize God's providence and care for his people and b) so that the Israelites would not forget where they came from (slavery) and what they had been elevated to (God's chosen people).

If you don't know who you are and your history, it becomes easy for anyone to dislodge you from your inheritance. Here a lie was propagated and promoted by the oppressor, and if that were accepted as the truth, then Israel would lose their existence, identity, and future in the promised land.

When a lie is presented as truth, such a belief can destroy your future. This is a trick used throughout human history to distract, discourage, and displace God's children. We see it in the garden of Eden. We see it in the response of the 10 Israelite spies. And we know the enemy is attempting to use that tactic again in Judges 11.

Here, history was presented as a lie with the motive to hurt and abuse others. The truth gives the people the power to fight against the lie that comes against them. Jephthah knew if the lie was accepted by the nations surrounding them, he would be viewed as a man who belonged to a group of people who oppressed, abused, and victimized people rather than a people who believed in bringing justice and peace. Jephthah had to know who he was and the facts about his history to defeat the enemy's attempt to frame him and his people as transgressors. The strategy to demean him and his people was done by causing fear, but there was a more extensive plan to destroy their future.

It was fear that drove the elders of Gilead to the son they'd rejected. It's also possible that, in their fear, they began to believe there may have been some truth to the Ammonite king's claims. Can fear make us believe in a lie as truth? The uncomfortable and sometimes devastating answer is yes.

Before he fought the physical battle, Jephthah engaged and won the mental battle with the power of his knowledge and his assurance in the Lord. The history of his people was the story of God. Though Jephthah was far from his home, he never doubted God and his people's account of God. His entire worldview and his entire identity were shaped and strengthened by it.

When our people hurt us, we often lose some part of our own story, and sometimes we even try to eliminate, distort, or change some details because it is difficult to include those who have hurt us as part of our story. That, again, can be a dangerous place to dwell.

Had Jephthah rejected those who'd hurt him or any part of his past, the battle against the Ammonites might have gone much differently. By remembering the legacy of his people in totality and in truth, Jephthah was also defending the name of God, who led them through such a journey—recalling that inheritance also gave him the strength to recognize that God who defeated the Ammonites once before would also defeat the Ammonites again. In remembering this, he rejected the lie that God was absent or unable to bring Israel to victory once again.

Confront the lie: *"Are you any better than Balak, Son of Zippor, king of Moab? Did he ever quarrel with Israel or fight with them?" —Judges 11:25*

Jephthah courageously fought the lie in his mind before he fought the physical battle. He knew who he was and what shaped him was his faith. He also knew the spiritual legacy he'd inherited; therefore, he spoke against the voice telling the untruth.

Too often, parents fail to address the lies their children have accepted and believed in, especially if they've allowed that lie to take root in their children's lives. They see a behavior issue and immediately go to war against it rather than seeking first to understand what has caused the behavior to begin with. A lack of interest in school is seen as a lack of direction or care for the future. The child may have accepted the lie that they will never live up to the impossible standards of perfection they believe their parents expect of them; thus, they've given up trying. So, the parents beg and plead and punish because they think they are acting in their child's best interest, and the child becomes depressed and more resentful because they believe their parents do not understand, love, or care for them.

Recently, school violence has increased to such an extent that many think it is an epidemic with no end. Every day, parents dread sending their children to school, which was once a place of safety, comfort, and peace. It is sad and depressing to see yet another story about a student who believed a lie was the truth and acted out of that belief system—to the distress and grief of all those around them.

Often, these students have felt rejected, unloved, and often ignored by their family and friends. They have experienced some form of bullying or ostracism, making them think that the world is a hateful place. Real or imagined, they cast themselves in the role of the outcast, and they eventually come to a place where they believe it is okay to go to war against those that they think have grievously wronged them. It doesn't matter who is innocent and who is guilty; all that matters is that they somehow believe they are justified and deserve to avenge themselves.

Who will confront this lie that many have come to believe? Who will reason with them and attempt to show them the truth?

It is important to note that Scripture has spoken the truth repeatedly that the enemy "comes to steal, kill and destroy," but the Son of Man has come so that we may "have life, and have it to the full" (John 10:10).

If we are to have victory over our hurts, it is essential to destroy the enemy's work that robs us of our peace and tries to kill our purpose by making us doubt the one who has come to save us—the one who came to give us abundant life through His sacrifice on the cross.

Uphold Justice and Truth: *"I have not wronged you, but you are doing me wrong by waging war against me. Let the Lord, the Judge, decide the dispute this day between the Israelites and the Ammonites." —Judges 11:27*

Jephthah makes his purpose clear when he prepares to fight the battle. He is there to fight the injustice a perpetrator is trying to stage against the weak. He doesn't allow a bully to have his way simply because he has chosen to walk in a lie that he believes somehow entitles him to his aggression.

Jephthah is courageous and unafraid to take up the cause of the weak. He doesn't feel threatened and faces the accuser, who tries to create fear in the victim's mind. He knows the truth is on his side because he has studied the facts and verified the history. He knows what he is doing—protecting the truth from the ones who are trying to distort that truth.

He also knows that giving his life for such a noble cause is worthwhile because he has not been deceived. He knows such an act will provide a future and hope to many children yet to be born. And he knows that if he is in the wrong in any way, God will make it known to him.

Finding the just cause, the just fight, and the right reason was significant for Jephthah. He chose to flee from his brothers in his youth rather than fight over his father's possessions because he recognized it was a fight that would only destroy his family. Now he wasn't just fighting for a claim for an earthly inheritance; he was fighting an enemy trying to steal something far more precious—the legacy of God's children. He knew the real warriors were the ones who lay down their lives for the salvation of many rather than fighting to enrich only themselves. Fighting was now his moral obligation.

A true warrior is not interested in simply winning a battle; a true warrior is willing to die to preserve the truth for the next generation. If Jephthah had not stood up, then the moral truth would have been lost from the pages of record, and, for the age to come, a lie would have found a place in history.

A warrior is not afraid to fight a battle that protects the truth—especially when that truth points directly back to our identities in God—so that the coming generation can find direction and strength for their battles.

Question for Reflection:

a. Do we sometimes make the battle all about us, our ego, and people's respect for us when the struggle is about who our God is and His plan and purpose for us? Share any story or specific experiences from your life.

6

Identity

"Now since the Lord, the God of Israel, has driven the Amorites out before his people Israel, what right have you to take it over? 24 Will you not take what your god Chemosh gives you? Likewise, whatever the Lord our God has given us, we will possess." —Judges 11:23–24

For better or worse, our identities and purpose are often tied to the land where we dwell. When traveling, one of the first questions we are asked is, "where are you from?" This is often followed by, "so, what do you do?" Based on those responses, the listener often makes a judgment call based on their own biases, interests, and experiences about whether you are worthy or unworthy of their continued time and attention.

Israel's identity and purpose were tied to the land they inhabited. It was more than a home; it signified God's promises to their forefathers and them. With the threat of the Ammonite armies looming over them, it wasn't just their claim to their land that was being challenged; their identity and purpose were also being challenged.

In the opening words of his letter to the Ephesians, the apostle Paul wrote, "Praise be to the God and Father of our Lord Jesus Christ, who has blessed us in the heavenly realms with every spiritual blessing in Christ" (Ephesians 1:3).

If you have placed your faith in Christ, the blessing Paul speaks of, and the responsibilities that come with it are already yours in Christ.

It is yours to keep! You own it. It has been given to you. You don't have to earn it. You don't have to work for it. It is a gift straight from the hand of God (Ephesians 2:8–9).

The only thing is, you are responsible for using that blessing—and the identity that comes with it—wisely. Therefore, you must safeguard it with all your heart. Your most significant role is protecting and keeping it safe from all who want to steal it from you.

Later in his letter, Paul warns the Ephesians that they must always be prepared for battle. As believers, we stand against a relentless enemy who will come at us with every trick to dislodge us from our place of promise. Scripture shows us that even those who begin with their identity and purpose firmly rooted in the Lord can lose sight of that promise and lose a battle that was theirs to win.

The events unfolding in Judges 11 were crucial moments in the history of the people of Israel. It was up to them not to sit silently while someone with a false claim stole their inheritance from under them. In order to stand firm, it is essential to know that the possession is given by God alone and that, unless you fully claim it, you could lose it. In his response to the king, Jephthah reminded his people to hold fast to the inheritance and possession of the land God had already granted them when He expelled its former occupants. He didn't want them to allow others to take over and claim what didn't belong to them. He knew God promised it, yet it had to be possessed by the people it was entrusted to.

Many of us are afraid to possess or take hold of the promises God has given us because we allow fear to fill our minds and spirits instead of God's peace. We go back and forth, questioning if what we have received or heard is ours to hold onto because we allow the enemy to whisper falsehoods and twisted truths into our ears.

James describes such a person as being "double-minded" and "unstable in all they do" (James 1:8). In other words, they're ineffective because they are ruled by doubt. They do not want to disturb the status quo or cause any trouble, avoiding conflict if possible—even if it means allowing wrongs to go unchallenged.

Jephthah knew it was essential to stand firm here because the Giver's reputation was on trial. The one who gave them the possession entrusted Jephthah and his people to manage it; to lose it meant the people accepted the enemy's lie that they were inferior to the way God saw them. Jephthah knew that God's thoughts and intentions for his people were only the best, and to uphold that trust, he had to do something. It was more about honoring what God believed about him and his people. It was about trusting God for what He entrusted him with. To give away the land to the Ammonites meant abandoning God's favor in exchange for man's favor. Ultimately, God's blessing was more valuable to him.

The lie the enemy came to Jephthah with removed God from the story of how they came to possess the land, and that took away the giver of the gift from the whole picture of history. Jephthah refused to remove God's rightful place from His story because God's position at the center of it all defined the past and the future of his people.

The Fight for Your Territory

How often does the enemy come to us to remove what we have been given possession of by removing God from our story? Once God is removed, it is easy to accept the lie that we are unworthy of being called God's child, of being called to work in a specific ministry or field, unworthy of being a parent or a spouse, unworthy of a gift or a talent—the list is endless.

Jephthah also understood that Israel couldn't possess such land in their strength apart from God. Without God fighting their battle, they would never have achieved what their fathers possessed. And it was vital for him to show his people that their strength was a gift given to them by their God, who loved them. So, it was essential for him to defend God in history and their story so that the people might know what they had received was a gift in the past, present, and future.

There is always a fight for what you have, more than who you are. What you possess will always be under attack because it is not ordinary. If it were expected, no one would bother about it. The reason people are after it is because they understand its value.

How often do we make the battle about us, our ego, and other people's respect for us when the struggle is about who our God is and His plan and purpose for us?

Look to the past when the enemy comes against your present and your future. Remember what God has done for you, the territories He has brought you into and cleared before you. When you are mindful of his place in your history, you will remain mindful of His rightful place in your present circumstances.

Stella was an extraordinary child who fought for her life from birth. Born with a defective heart, Stella suffered much for one so young. But her mother knew she was a unique child, not because of her medical needs, but because of who she was and how much she meant to her mother. She knew her child would be extraordinary when she laid eyes on her beautiful daughter. Indeed, she came with a heavy price because on the day she was born, the doctors didn't know if Stella would survive even the first hour. But Stella overcame the difficult period, surprising them all.

Many friends who came to see Stella later marveled at her tenacity, and every time the doctors gave a reason why she should not live, Stella proved otherwise. It was like she wanted to be here for a reason. Her mother knew it, and she was willing to go to any extent to ensure her child's well-being.

It was hard for both parents, going in and out of the hospital for most of the initial years of their baby's life. They watched her learn to breathe on her own without a machine; they watched her develop cognitively, like any other baby, becoming more and more aware of the world around her. All they have endured and gone through was worth it, but there was one small thing.

One minor medical condition stunted Stella's growth, preventing her from growing beyond a few centimeters; her body remained the size of an infant. Still, her mother didn't give up. She knew Stella was a gift from God and knew that what she was going through would serve a greater purpose. One beyond what she could see.

Initially, comprehending it all was a real challenge, but through the years, they learned to be grateful for every moment they had with Stella. They knew beyond a doubt that God gave them a baby with such a complication because He would be glorified through it, and Stella's life would be a blessing that far outweighed her health challenges.

Though Stella is now a teenager and still has a few life-threatening medical issues, she has survived. Though her body has not grown beyond the size of a few-months-old baby, she is full of life and spirit. Her parents are reminded each day how this child of theirs has made them special parents. Though many don't understand how God could allow such hardship, this child has given her family great hope, joy, and strength they would have otherwise never known.

When life hands us difficulties like Stella's, it's easier to sit back, question where God is, and think if He has just abandoned us. It's harder and more praiseworthy to stand firm in our faith, to trust in God's promises and steadfast presence. Stella's parents believed that what they were given was a gift from above through their daughter, and they claimed it with every fiber of their being. In the same way, Jephthah took firm hold of what God had entrusted him with and refused to give in to the enemy's demands.

Eventually, Israel would lose sight of God's promise and place in their history. They would turn to false gods and mercenary armies to protect them from those coming against them. Eventually, they would lose their possession of the land and become scattered throughout enemy empires. But even then, God's promise to save and redeem his lost sheep remained.

In his opening letter to the "twelve tribes scattered among the nations," James wrote: *Consider it pure joy whenever you face trials of many kinds because you know that testing your faith produces perseverance. Let perseverance finish its work so that you may be mature and complete, not lacking anything (James 1:2–3).*

When the enemy comes, trying to convince you to give up what God has entrusted you with, do you choose to stand firm in the possession and blessing God has given you? Or does your heart fail you, leading you to relinquish your place to another?

The trials are seldom easy and rarely enjoyable, but we are told repeatedly throughout Scripture to "fear not." When our eyes are fixed on Christ and His promises, which we have been given in Him; we are filled with a peace—an assurance—that "transcends all understanding" and guards our hearts and minds against the lies and fears the enemy tries to fill our ears with (Philippians 4:7).

A true warrior gains victory and possesses the prize not because of their strength or character but because of the power of the Lord, which is given to all who are in Christ and hold firm to the promises of God.

Questions for Reflection:

a. The lie the enemy came to Jephthah removed God from the story of how they came to possess the land. What are some lies you see that try to eliminate God within your life, community, or your culture?

b. Are there some battles you are engaged in where the enemy is trying to take away the things that rightfully belong to you from God?

7

Win & Lose

And Jephthah made a vow to the Lord: "If you give the Ammonites into my hands, whatever comes out of the door of my house to meet me when I return in triumph from the Ammonites will be the Lord's, and I will sacrifice it as a burnt offering." Then Jephthah went over to fight the Ammonites, and the Lord gave them into his hands. —Judges 11:30–31

Turning a great victory into a great tragedy can take only a moment. Even a great warrior who can conquer and accomplish an incredible feat can lose everything if they miss one opportunity to trust in the Lord.

Up to this point, Jephthah has done well. He has asked the right questions, he has given the correct responses, and everything that has unfolded—from his brothers coming to him, hat in hand, and making him their leader to presenting a path to peace to his enemy—has shown him that he has the Lord's favor and permission to take the next step. Whether it was a moment of passionate zeal or self-doubt before the battle began in earnest, Jephthah made a foolish vow.

This man, who knew the history of his people and the place God had in it, made an open-ended bargain that is not reflected in any of the Lord's worship directions. In his haste, he first failed to consult the Lord or any of the priests before making his promise; he also could not consider the consequences of such a vow—both for himself and the people he'd been called to lead.

Jephthah—and anyone who hears his story—is given every indication that God had already given the Ammonites into Jephthah's hand. Because the battle was the Lord's, victory was assured without vows or bargains.

Yet, in one moment of pride or fear, that victory would become tainted for all generations.

Doctor Christopher was known for his heart and commitment to the people he served in the inner city of a developing nation. Arriving at his clinic early in the morning, he would examine his patients with the utmost care and attention until after dark. To him, each of his patients represented life in need of special care, and he felt he was called to make sure that they left his clinic better than they came in.

Dr. Chris himself had a humble background. He grew up in an inner city in utter poverty yet excelled in his studies and later went to the West to develop his surgical skills. When he returned after completing his higher studies, he was eager to serve the needy. Over the years, his practice grew from a small clinic serving under twenty patients daily to a multi-specialty downtown facility with beds for over a hundred patients. He moved his small family closer to the hospital to be more available to his patients.

There was something different about "Dr. Chris," as he was called so fondly by his patients. He often waved off his fees when he knew the people couldn't afford even the low and essential treatment cost. For him, serving the people was a more crucial calling than making a lavish living.

While he found much meaning in his work, the time he dedicated to his work came with a price. Though his family loved him much and supported his tireless work, they felt neglected and ignored. They were the ones who had to pay a heavy price for their service to others. Apart from being absent from the home for long hours, he was rarely available for his children and never present for any school functions, graduations, and birthdays.

Dr. Chris justified his actions by saying that everything he did was for the people and their service. His life was spent caring for those who left his family without a husband or a father. It was okay when his two girls were little, but as they grew up, they rebelled and didn't have anything to do with him or what he was doing. After finishing high school, his girls left home and started working far away. Rarely would they come and visit their parents.

Thrice abandoned, this devastated his wife. She didn't have anywhere else to go, nor did she have any other purpose for living. She had no friends, children, and grandchildren running about her feet and no life partner. All she had for a relationship was another tired body resting in the same bed during the wee hours of the night after her husband came home to eat the cold dinner and crawl under the blankets beside her.

Dr. Chris didn't know that his wife was battling a deep depression that would one day claim her life. But the greatest tragedy was that no one knew she had killed herself until the following day. Dr. Chris, who didn't see her at the breakfast table, found his wife's lifeless body hanging from the ceiling. He'd been too tired after coming home the night before to notice that she wasn't beside him in the bed.

These days he can still be found in the hospital, but he looks frail and tired. He helped many others but couldn't help his own. Though Dr. Chris was faithful in his work and service, it came with a heavy price that cost him what was most precious in the end.

When claiming our calling, we must be careful to recognize that God doesn't beckon us to walk beside him at the expense of our family. We must be cautious so that we do not become so fixated on our work in our zeal to serve that we fail to care for and protect the family he has gifted us. When we don't, our most significant victories can quickly be overshadowed by tragedy.

The door of My House

When Jephthah returned to his home in Mizpah, who should come out to meet him but his daughter, dancing to the sound of timbrels! She was an only child. Except for her, he had neither Son nor daughter. When he saw her, he tore his clothes and cried, "Oh no, my daughter! You have brought me down, and I am devastated. I have made a vow to the Lord that I cannot break." —Judges 11:34–35

Here Jephthah had won one of the most significant victories for Israel. He fought an intense battle and overcame an enemy that had been unjustly harassing the people in Gilead for 18 years (Judges 10:8), but when he came home to celebrate his victory, it turned out to be one of the most tragic days in his life. What should greet him and thus be subject to his rash vow in the heat of battle, but his daughter and only child?

Of all the things to offer to the Lord, why would Jephthah provide as a burnt offering whatever came out of the door of his house to meet him when he returned in triumph (Judges 11:31)?

An oath made by suppressed pain

When we look back at his early life, we are reminded that he was driven out of his own home—for which he was never given an apology. Even when addressing his grievance to the community's elders by saying, "Don't you remember that I was driven out of the house by your hate?" (v. 7), his wound was brushed off in their response, Forget the past as we have. Aren't we choosing you as our leader now? They only had to say: "Nevertheless, we are turning to you now; (v. 8).

When old wounds are ignored and brushed aside by us or those who have wounded us, the grief can return to trip us up and mar the future God promised us. Even though power, position, and respect came to him, there may still have been a part of him that felt unworthy as the formerly rejected Son born out of an illegitimate and sinful union. His oath may have come out of that wound as a promise to make a final break from his past hurts, but the Scriptures are silent on this matter. What we do know is that his oath came back to haunt him.

His daughter was his only child; she meant everything to him. She was his security and future, the one who was innocent and beautiful and needed protection— everything he had needed in his childhood but was denied. He'd worked hard to build it back and provide a better life for his family, but everything fell apart when his daughter came dancing out the door.

Jephthah's cry at seeing his daughter shows us the recognition of his rash act has come too late. His pride has been humbled, his life turned to rubble, because above all else, he was a man of his word, and he knew that the words he'd spoken to God—whatever the rationale behind it—could not be taken back.

The enemy knows our hurts and our griefs; he knows what buttons to push, what puffs up our egos, and what can send us spiraling into depression. He looks for openings in our lives where he can put that knowledge to use to prevent us from stepping into the complete victory that God intends for us to walk in. This is why it is essential to make peace with our pain and resolve our severe issues before they can come back and harm us and those we love.

Jephthah was a mighty warrior, but a war was going on within him. His response to the elders when they came to him reveals that the pain of being "driven out from his father's house" was still a significant part of who he was. None of the successes or the power and positions could heal his wounds. Only forgiving the debt owed by those who had wronged him and accepting the promise of the one who had raised him up could do that.

Or was there a part deep within him that always felt shameful because of who he was (son of a prostitute), which made him feel unworthy to receive the victory (or anything good) without offering something back to God? Paying to God for his goodness and grace could be coming from a place within him that felt he was incapable of obtaining anything good in life. Whatever it was, the oath came out of a dark place and burnt everything.

It is essential to know that what we avoid can become a more significant issue if we are not careful. If we are to rise above our hurts into greatness, we must first accept that a healed heart that has recognized and resolved the deep wounds of our past and can receive the grace of God is necessary to protect and ensure our future. Yes, elders, counselors, and physicians can aid us in that journey, but true, complete healing, forgiveness, and acceptance must come from the Lord.

Sherwin was a promising young pastor with a passionate spirit and a fantastic gift of communication. He significantly influenced the young generation and built a vital congregation where thousands of people gathered weekly to listen to him. Many people confessed to finding meaning and experiencing fundamental transformation within themselves by being part of this spiritual community.

His church was known to be an oasis where hurting people enduring difficult times found peace, strength, and a caring community. Sherwin also developed a large following on social media, where people downloaded most of his sermons and bought many of his sermon podcasts. He was a celebrity until one Sunday morning, his assistant, the executive pastor, stepped up the podium. There he read Sherwin's letter, written as the parting words to his congregation and to his online friends. Out of nowhere, this much-acclaimed pastor decided to leave the ministry, fame, and everything he had built and was known for to seek guidance and healing.

In the days that followed, many facts came out. One that hurt and shocked the people most was the pastor's addiction to alcohol, which he had battled for some time. There was another allegation of unfaithfulness with finances.

It was later revealed that his father had committed suicide when he was a young boy, and in the subsequent years, Sherwin had endured many hardships, including living on the street for some years. None of this had ever been shared with the congregation before. They knew only the successful minister and never saw the deep wounds he'd kept hidden for so long. In the end, the fame, the popularity, and even the paycheck couldn't dull the unresolved grief, which continued to gnaw at him until he finally sought refuge in drinking to numb himself to the pain.

The Ultimate Victory: Forgiveness

"My father," she replied, "you have given your word to the Lord. Do to me just as you promised, now that the Lord has avenged you of your enemies, the Ammonites. But grant me this one request," she said. "Give me two months to roam the hills and weep with my friends, because I will never marry" —Judges 11:36–37)

The closing scene of Jephthah's story can lead to an endless debate: Who was responsible for the child's death? Was it Jephthah for preserving his honor rather than preserving his child? Was it God who did not stay Jephthah's hand as he had Abraham's?

Ultimately, I feel the daughter was killed on the altar because of her father's unbelief, insecurity, fear, and ego. She was so young and didn't have to die in such a way at that time. All she wanted was to celebrate and participate in her father's accomplishments. She wanted to be by her father's side in his joyous moment. She tried to tell him that she was proud of him and all his accomplishments.

But that never happened. Before she could speak, her father told her that she made him desperate and sorrowful. He effectively placed his pain and the blame for her death at her own feet.

Anger and horror aside, if we focus on who carries the blame for the young girl's death, we will miss out on a critical moment in which the act of a nameless child becomes immortalized forever.

After hearing her father's words, Jephthah's daughter could have rebelled and fled, attempting to find safety in another city, a Tob, among different people (like her father, Jephthah did in response to towards his father's mistake). She could have begged, pleaded, and tried to reason with her father. Instead, her words remind us of another virgin who, hundreds of years later, would also submit herself to her father's promise, regardless of what it could mean for her future (Luke 1:38).

Jephthah's daughter's response also indicates her forgiveness to her father for his rash words and future actions, thus breaking the cycle of brokenness that has thus far been passed from one generation to the next. Instead, she entirely entrusted herself to the Lord, grieving what would never be and then submitting herself to be the sacrifice.

There is no recorded mention that the people celebrated Jephthah's victory over the Ammonites. Instead, it is said the young women of Israel would "go out for four days to commemorate the daughter of Jephthah the Gileadite" from that day on (v. 40). Instead of being reminded of his victory, we are reminded of her sacrifice.

Jephthah's story acts as a mirror for us to hold up and judge ourselves by. How often do we end up hurting the innocent without taking responsibility for our mistakes, especially as fathers? Jephthah's *father's sin* was a purely carnal action, while Jephthah's was wrapped up in the guise of spirituality. In both cases, it was ultimately their children who suffered.

Perhaps God uses this story to warn us of the sins repeated within our homes when we do not deal with them in our lifetime. In time, those secret sins become more deeply entrenched and difficult to break free of, affecting the family and the community. We see this in the response of the daughter and her friends. Instead of celebrating her coming of age and her eventual marriage, they retreat for two months to grieve her coming death and the loss that it represents for the entire village. In the end, no one was spared the pain of her death.

What do we do when the people we look up to abandon and betray us through their selfish acts or unhealed wounds? Do we use their actions to justify our own? Do we continue in unforgiveness, suppressing our anger or putting it on full display for others to see until we are destroyed relationally, physically, or professionally?

Or do we lay the sins committed against us at the feet of our God along with the sins we had committed, as Christ taught us to do when He instructed his disciples how to pray (Matthew 6:12)?

When we choose the latter, God not only brings us into a place of healing, but He also safeguards us from the temptation of thinking of ourselves more highly than we ought to, thus delivering us from the evil one who seeks to bring us down into grief when we ought to be celebrating a great victory.

Questions for Reflection:

a. What do you feel about the vow Jephthah made to God? Was it right to sacrifice his daughter? What are some vows or religious beliefs that are harmful within your community?

b. Have you ever felt the people you looked up to abandoned and betrayed you through their selfish acts or unhealed wounds? What do you do then?

c. Have you ever used their actions to justify your own?

James Levi

8

Wisdom of Elders

Sometime later, when the Ammonites were fighting against Israel, the elders of Gilead went to get Jephthah from the land of Tob. "Come," they said, "be our commander, so we can fight the Ammonites." —Judges 11:4

In ancient cultures, the elders in the community were primarily older men who served as leaders or rulers. People could bring their disputes to them, seek advice, or counsel, and often look to them for spiritual guidance. After the formation of the Christian Church, elders were selected from mature members of the faith to serve as the spiritual overseers of each congregation, as for the first time in Acts 6:1–4 and laid out by the apostle Paul for the Gentile churches in 1 Timothy 5 and Titus 1:5–9.

Then as well as now, one of the chief responsibilities of an elder was to bring the community together and direct them to move forward in unity, following the commands of the Lord. We see the elders fulfilling this role in Judges 11 when they came to Tob to bring home a lost son.

Despite how Japheth's story ends, his story happened because of the wise counsel of some elders. If they had not boldly moved and taken some critical steps, the life of Jephthah would have taken a completely different route, and their community would have been at risk of further plundering and destruction by the Ammonites. They were the ones who intervened when the communication between Jephthah and his brothers was broken beyond hope of repair.

They recognized an urgent need for someone to take charge and defend their people and the elders had the wisdom and ability to identify the right person for the job. Rather than watching their lands get stolen and their homes destroyed, they were willing to do what it took to step into a familial conflict and bring the war between the brothers to an end.

It may not have been an easy decision to bring back Jephthah, who had been driven away by their people, and Jephthah himself was hurt and bitter after being forced to live far away from home. Yet they were willing to take that risk of going to him to convince him to come back.

Even though Jephthah was a mighty warrior still, he was forgotten by his people; he was driven away from his destiny, removed from his purpose, and without a part to play in the land of Israel. He would have been a lost hero without the courageous work of the elders.

Although no formal apology was given for the community's actions against Jephthah, it is essential to note that the elders were the ones who connected him back to his original purpose and gave him the objective to complete his calling. The elders' active role saved an entire community from the enemy's attack.

My Mentor: Dr. Kietzman was in his late eighties when I first met him. It was by pure chance that I saw him in his office, and my brief and formal meetings with this pleasant and insightful person forever changed my life. I didn't know it then, but his voice and spirit would move me from a place of discouragement to a place of hope and strength.

I had finished my master's level studies at a good university in the US and was looking to complete my doctoral program. I was interested in researching leadership and community growth. Coming from a third-world country, I have seen the effects a disconnected and unconcerned administration can have on the lives of ordinary people. But I didn't have a mentor in my life, nor did I believe someone would be interested in seeing me succeed or see my dream come to reality.

It was a period where I felt that much of what I was doing was a waste, and it would be hard to break through in an environment that was too competitive and expensive. But my meeting with Dr. Kietzman changed everything because he was willing to hear me out and see things through a very different lens as I talked to him.

He didn't have the bias and the prejudice I had about myself. I was in a place where I didn't see myself being able to do doctoral-level studies, but once I allowed my mentor's words to sink into my heart, I was instantly filled with a new hope. It was not the situation around me that changed but my perspective. My future, which looked bleak when I entered his office, suddenly opened up with new possibilities.

Dr. Kietzman believes in me and for me. From his position and experience, he could see a future for me that I could not. It was a journey, and for the next few years, God helped me to allow the wisdom of this great man to continue to speak into my life. I grasped the faith that God poured into me, and I began seeing what Dr. Kietzman had seen. Soon the things that had once seemed impossible for me became not only possibilities but reality.

Now I know how important it is to allow the voice of wisdom to speak into our lives when things are dark and hopeless. Not only that, but my prayer has also been to become a voice of healing and comfort to those who are going through similar difficulties. I hope to see a positive future in the lives of people for whom things have been challenging and hostile and robbed them of the ability to see themselves as God sees them, fully capable of doing tremendous things in his name and his strength.

We note that the elders here possessed immense wisdom and were experienced people who could know people's strengths within their community. They could see the warrior spirit of Jephthah, even though he was driven out of their home and was not living among them. That didn't keep them from reaching out to the person who would be their savior.

They were the people who did not stop pursuing the warriors among them even when the environment around them was not conducive or favorable. They went searching for the one who was lost from them because they knew who he was and what they lacked without him. When others were willing to give up on Jephthah because of his past and background, these elders would rise above the ordinary. They could see what was essential and suitable for that crucial historical moment. If they had given in to what the family had believed about Jephthah, they wouldn't have taken that extra effort to bring him back from a faraway land.

Faithful elders come to their decisions without bias and look for ways to bring healing and reconciliation to fractured societal relationships. They mentor the young, regardless of their background or status, and help them to move boldly into their future and where the young men and women, in turn, can take those critical steps that strengthen and preserve their community.

With all the roles the elders played in restoring Jephthah to this warrior position and thus helping bring victory to the people of Israel, there is a definite lack on their part in saving the daughter's life. It is sad to see that they did not counsel or help Jephthah in protecting the girl. Was it that they went to fetch Jephthah for their own need because their life was under threat from the enemy, but when it came to the death of a girl, they didn't lose anything and thus didn't interfere? What does it say about the elders? Why does it always have to be that we do things to protect ourselves and care for ourselves while ignoring things that affect the lives of others?

The Role of the Elders

Since an overseer manages God's household, he must be blameless—not overbearing, not quick-tempered, not given to drunkenness, not violent, and not pursuing dishonest gain. Rather, he must be hospitable, one who loves what is good, who is self-controlled, upright, holy, and disciplined. He must hold firmly to the trustworthy message as it has been taught so that he can encourage others with sound doctrine and refute those who oppose it. —Titus 1:7–9

Godly elders often see things in a very different light than other members of society, as we can see here in the story. Jephthah, though he was a warrior, was hurt and had suffered a lot at the hands of the people, so for him, it was impossible to see him ever leading his people. Even in his wildest dreams, he didn't have the strength to dream of becoming the leader of his tribe because he knew how his brothers hated him. His pain was real, and his wounds were deep and unhealed, which kept him from seeing what these elders were seeing.

At the same time, Jephthah's family was so close to their pain and sense of betrayal that they could never accept Jephthah as one of them. To them, he was a dark spot in their family's bright and shining reputation. They could not see him being a leader of God's holy people when his mother was a prostitute.

This shame and bias prevented his people from seeing beyond what was culturally and socially acceptable to what God was doing to redeem his people. They may have been willing to perish at the hands of the enemies before accepting a person with such a past to save them, but the elders could see beyond their clouded judgment and brought a new vision and clarity to the situation. They engaged with a hurt person and moved beyond those who had hurt him to bring healing. This kind of insight most often comes through wisdom combined with personal experience. These elders made a difference because they were willing to step into their role as peacemakers rather than attempting to be peacekeepers, whose only goal was maintaining the status quo.

When looking at elders, there are three things to consider:

a. Are they able to assess the problem clearly and prayerfully seek the Lord's wisdom in responding in a manner that brings a resolution while honoring God?

b. Do they protect the warriors by speaking words of truth and healing into their lives and prompting them to step into the work the Lord has called them to?

c. And finally, do they work to promote unity within the community through their lived-out examples of righteous living and seeking out those who have been lost or waylaid? Can they rise above their fears and selfish agendas to protect innocent lives?

Sally was the only child and the joy of her parents, who had her in the very late years of their life. They were lavish parents who gave their child everything she asked for or dreamed about. Slowly but surely, their doting and permissiveness resulted in a spoiled child who was ill-prepared for the realities of life.

When she was a teenager, Sally continued to act as if she were a young child. She'd learned that when she whined more, her parents gave in to her and that if she made a fuss, she would always get her way. When she reached school age, she was shocked that her teachers and peers would not respond to her in the same way.

Unhappy with how "unfairly" she was being treated, Sally dropped out of school during her teen years, and when her parents objected, she made a scene. As was their habit, they accepted her wishes though it was an embarrassment. Then she refused to do any chores at home, nor did she plan to go out and earn a living. She fully expected her parents to cater to her every need.

This went on for an extended period, bringing untold misery and heartache to her poor, aging parents, who could think of no way to resolve the situation they found themselves in. All of it changed once her grandmother came to live with them. Sally's grandmother was a woman who was short in stature but high in wisdom. She quickly assessed the situation carefully and recognized what needed to be done to bring healing.

Though she was old and weak, she wouldn't sit there and allow the destruction of her family to happen on her watch. Soon she started bringing both parties to engage in a conversation that could have gone better. Despite the opposition, the grandmother continued to take charge and listened to her children and grandchild. And she was able to advise accordingly.

Soon Sally began to see the trouble she was bringing on herself and her parents because of her selfishness and stubbornness. In time, she moved into one of her friend's basement apartments. In return for the rent, she babysat the friend's two children. She also joined the community college and began training to become a hairstylist.

It took over a year before Sally could find a decent job, live on her own, and rent a good apartment. It was hard initially, but it brought her a sense of worth and confidence that she didn't have before. With a new life, Sally could also see how she needed her grandmother's wisdom more, so she reconnected with her family in a healthy relationship that both honored her parents and allowed them to treat her with the dignity and respect of a grown woman.

A grandmother's wisdom allowed her to see the problem clearly and enabled her to speak into both her children's and grandchildren's lives. Her patience and care brought healing and restoration to the family and enabled an aimless young girl to rise and become a woman with dignity and purpose.

The Mission of the Elders

So, Jephthah went with the elders of Gilead, and the people made him head and commander over them. And he repeated all his words before the Lord in Mizpah. —Judges 11:11

The elders from Gilead saved the people from the hands of the enemy by bringing back Jephthah to fight the battle and reconnected Jephthah to his true calling and purpose. Without their intervention, Jephthah may have spent his entire life running around with that gang of scoundrels who had started following him. Because of their right action, the people could fight the enemy and win the battle.

Without their intervention, Gilead's victory was a distant dream. These elders brought confidence and faith back to the people and gave them a new future.

But for all of their wisdom, the choice to step into his future remained with Jephthah. In the end, he chose to listen to his elders, follow their counsel, and work for the benefit of everyone. Likewise, elders are still living and present in our communities. Like Jephthah, it is up to us to make time and space for them to speak into our lives.

As you allow God to raise you out of your hurt and into the greatness, He has called you into, remember the people who have helped shape the success of your community. They have wisdom you can learn from. Remember those who have played an essential role in your personal and spiritual growth and acknowledge them. And remember the mentors who have spoken unseen truths over you that have encouraged you to take that next step.

In time, we may find ourselves where we are called to act as the elders in our community. If we are to have success first as warriors and then as elders, we must continually endeavor to seek out God's will for our community so that we can lead and advise others in their time of great need.

Questions for Reflection:

a. Do you see that the wisdom of the elders is appreciated in our community?

b. Who are God's elders in your life to bring you back to your destiny?

c. Do you feel God is calling you to be a mentor or a voice of wisdom in the lives of those cast out or marginalized from your community?

James Levi

ABOUT THE AUTHOR

James Levi, Ph.D., is a Christian minister who regularly conducts retreats and workshops. He is also the author of 38 at Estelle, The Living Clay, The Seventh Man, Visible Faith, Unholy Worshipper, Higher Ground, and Talitha Koum. He is a licensed pilot who loves brewing coffee for his friends and family. Learn more about the author, his books, by visiting the website www.jameslevi.org.